MODERNITY, GLOBALIZATION AND IDENTITY

Towards A Reflexive Quest

MODERNITY, GLOBALIZATION AND IDENTITY

Towards A Reflexive Quest

AVIJIT PATHAK

MODERNITY, GLOBALIZATION AND IDENTITY
Avijit Pathak

First Published 2006
Reprinted 2008
Reprinted 2011
Reprinted 2018

ISBN 978-81-87879-62-6

Published by
AAKAR BOOKS
28 E Pocket IV, Mayur Vihar Phase I
Delhi 110 091, India
aakarbooks@gmail.com
www.aakarbooks.com

Printed at
Sapra Brother, Delhi 110 092

To Nutan for eternal bliss

Contents

Preface

There are primarily three questions that have led me to engage in a self-reflexive exercise, and write this book. The questions that strike me—and, as I guess, many of my readers—are:

1. Is it possible not to be overshadowed by the promises and achievements of a ruthlessly assertive modernity? Or, is it possible to alter its character, and to make it more humane, introspective and self-critical?
2. Can we evolve an art of resistance to overcome the unevenness in the prevalent practice of globalization, and create a situation conducive to a more dialogic cross-cultural conversation?
3. How do we grow more inclusive and open, and overcome the limitedness of social identities emanating from caste, ethnicity, gender, language, nationality and religion?

These questions are not discrete and discontinuous. There is an organic link. Modernity has acquired a new meaning in the global era. And culture-specific identities, far from withering away, are redefining their roles. In fact, to throw light on these queries is to throw light on our collective destiny characterized by modernity, global networking and identity politics. Enough has already been said and written on this fast-changing social landscape. This splendid scholarship makes me humble. I realize that mine is only a humble effort to contribute to this ongoing quest. What, however, gives a distinctive character to the book is its sensitivity to the social reality in India, and its urge to enrich itself through social theories, everyday experiences and even autobiographical reflections.

The specialized sub-culture of the university, its academic discourses and its specific research style do have an impact on me. Yet, in this book, as readers would notice, I have tried my best to minimize this influence. I am not a 'detached', 'value-neutral', 'scientific' observer. I have not withdrawn myself—my own experience, my vulnerability, my politics—from the text. Instead, I have relied heavily on *self-reflexivity*. The reason is that in the process of knowing the world out there, I need to know myself, and acknowledge my own experiences. Knowing myself and knowing the world are not two different things. The book, therefore, does not look like a disembodied/technical document. It is more like a narrative that seeks to reconcile subjectivity and objectivity, ideal and real, poetry and science, and sociology as a fact and creative existence as a possibility. My 'I' is distinctively visible in the text. Yet, it is not a narcissistic, atomized and insulated 'I'. My story, I like to believe, is also the story of my readers. That is why, I have chosen to write this book. My goal is to communicate with the larger audience—social scientists, researchers, students, activists and all those who believe that the questions we raise, far from being purely academic, are related to the very art of living.

Teaching, I have always felt, is a perpetual process of learning. As a vocation it enables me to expand my horizon, and appreciate new ideas and sensibilities. Furthermore, the dialogic milieu prevalent in the Jawaharlal Nehru University makes me vibrant and alive. I am indeed grateful to my students and colleagues. And my family members have always inspired me, and given me the confidence to believe that life is a celebration of grand ideals. I realize that this book is not just my book; it emerges out of this shared dream.

September 2005

Avijit Pathak
Jawaharlal Nehru University
New Delhi

1

Feasibility of Another Modernity

Enough has already been said and written about sociology—its critical engagement with modernity: the modernity that emerged in the West at a crucial juncture of its history. It was often said that Enlightenment philosophers were laying the foundation of a liberal/rational/secular order. And sociology as it evolved—from Comte's law of three stages to Marx's historical materialism—taught us diverse ways of looking at the post-Enlightenment era. Durkheim saw growing differentiation, specialization, division of labour and resultant organic solidarity in modern industrial societies. Weber saw the process of rationalization, or the emergence of a bureaucratic form of authority in the new age. And Marx saw capitalism, its market economy, and its inherent contradictions. Not solely that. With the passage of time, sociologists—particularly the adherents of post-modernity—began to critique the very foundation of Enlightenment modernity. In a way, as I see, my growing up with sociology is like engaging myself with modernity (Pathak, 2004).

It is also important to look at my own location in history. Yes, the colonial state—with its economic policies, its administrative and legal network, its English education, and its improved modes of transportation and communication—did give us the structure of modernity. But then, the experience of colonial modernity—because of its innate violence, asymmetry and exploitativeness, and its arrogance and skepticism towards our own cultural practices—was often traumatic. What is, however, interesting to note is that after a prolonged struggle for decolonization the agenda of nation-making that we initiated was filled with the same ethos of optimism which was derived from the principles of modernity. It was like believing in the doctrine of techno-industrial progress, in a secular state acting as a modernizing agency, and in a 'nation' that brings political centrality and order amidst cultural diversity. Yet, with the passage of time we witnessed innumerable anomalies and contradictions. The crisis in the secular foundation of the state, the growing identity politics, the political articulation of differences, the environmental movements, and multiple voices emanating from the marginalized communities began to cause a severe challenge to the grand agenda of modernity: its centrality, and its language of science, development and progress. Not solely that. We also became aware of the specificity of our own modernity: something that is different from mere Westernization, and is rooted in our own cultural history.

The project of modernity, needless to add, has become a site of intellectual/academic debate. We see the proliferation of books and literature produced by hardcore modernists, postcolonial theorists, postmodernists, environmentalists, Gandhians and feminists. But what I wish to emphasize is that my interest in modernity is not merely academic and cognitive. It is also experiential, and to a great extent, self-reflexive. Modernity, as I would substantiate, is about contradictory and conflicting experiences. Yes, there are positive experiences relating to the spirit of freedom, criticality and agency. And there are also painful experiences relating to existential and cultural anguish. These experiences arouse my interest in modernity. In other words, my engagement with modernity is sociological, historical and experiential. And possibly, out of these complex experiences emerges my urge to think of an alternative/life-affirming modernity.

I
Core Values of Modernity

There are many definitions of modernity. And there are many culture-specific articulations of modernity. These diverse projects of modernity notwithstanding, there is a set of core values which, I believe, every adherent of modernity seeks to privilege. And possibly even the most adamant critics of modernity would find it difficult to negate the liberating potential of these values. To begin with, I wish to speak of these positive experiences of modernity. Modernity, its adherents argue, is invariably related to the spirit of freedom. This freedom is rooted in the *critical consciousness* that it generates. It means: 'Don't take things for granted. Question it, verify it, and subject everything to critical scrutiny'. There is nothing which is beyond critical examination. Instead, everything—including the most sacred—has to be observed, verified and interrogated. No wonder, this fundamental Enlightenment spirit which was evolved through the historic Renaissance and Reformation, broke the static/taken for granted world: a world often legitimated by social customs, religious sanctions and an institutionalized divine order. This breakdown led to the ever-expanding discoveries, innovations and experimentations in every field of social life. In a way, modernity gave one the confidence to question the most cherished/established beliefs, and propose new ideas. This freedom from orthodoxy—or the freedom to question, and explore new ideas—is indeed a great achievement of modernity. In the modern age, as Eisenstadt would have argued, 'the sanctity and status quo of the past—of any past—as the major symbolic regulator of social, political and cultural change and innovation, has given way to the acceptance of innovation and orientation to the future as a basic dimension of cultural orientation'.(Eisenstadt, 1987:6). It is in this sense that we see modernity in Galileo when he questioned the religious belief regarding the centrality of the earth in the universe. We see modernity in Luther and Calvin. And we see modernity in Rammohun Roy when he fought against orthodox pandits, and pleaded for a ban on the practice of *sati*. We see modernity in B.R. Ambedkar when he burnt a copy of the *Manusmriti*, and raised his dissenting voice against the age-old caste system. And we see modernity in young Gandhi when he disobeyed the verdict of the caste association, and chose to visit abroad. In other words, modernity, because of this critical or Kantian thrust, is experienced as an *emancipatory* quest which, it is argued, is qualitatively different from the taboos of traditionalism. Indeed, in everyday life modernity is often celebrated as freedom: when, to use analogies from our own society, a young girl from rural India commits herself to a cross-religious marriage, or a young boy from Bihar overcomes the parental pressure, refuses to accept dowry, and chooses his life-partner from an altogether different community. Possibly it is this new aspiration that Daniel Lerner too talked about while celebrating 'the passing of traditional society'. A traditional man, as Lerner argued, tends to reject innovation by saying: 'It has never been thus', whereas one who is modern is more likely to ask 'Does it work?' and try the new way without much ado (Lerner, 2000:122). Even though Lerner's dichotomy of tradition vs. modernity is simplistic, it is difficult to deny the spirit of freedom that man cherishes—and cherishes more frequently—in the new age.

Another associated gain of modernity is that it opens up the world. It brings intense dynamism, arouses tremendous vertical/horizontal mobility, and gives us a wide-ranging exposure. The reason is that its inherent criticality leads to diverse experimentations and life-projects. Nothing remains static and stable. Change/innovation tends to characterize the spirit of modernity. No wonder, with modernization it becomes exceedingly difficult to retain a small, closed, homogeneous and well-insulated community.

Instead, as sociologists and cultural anthropologists have repeatedly pointed out, we witness a shift from a small, kinship-oriented, tradition-centric community to a vast heterogeneous/innovative society. True, this shift could not be easy, smooth and linear. There would be pathos, tensions and resistance. We know that Comte did not appreciate the growing individualism in his time. He sought to restore 'moral communities'. Durkheim was equally concerned with the growing *anomic* disorder is modern societies. In other words, as Robert Nisbet has suggested, the concern for stable/cohesive communities did not escape the attention of the sociologists who were otherwise modern (Nisbet, 1967). But then, the point I am trying to put forward is that modernity does essentially open up the world, and make us encounter what Peter L Berger would regard as the 'plurality of life-words':

> Compared with modern societies, most earlier ones evinced a high degree of integration. Whatever the differences between various sectors of social life, these would hang together in an order of integrating meaning that included them all. The integrating order was typically religious. For the individual this meant quite simply that the *same* integrative symbols permeated the various sectors of his everyday life. Whether with his family or at work or engaged in political processes or participating in festivity and ceremonial, the individual was always in the same 'world'. . . The typical situation on individuals in a modern society is very different. Different sectors of their everyday life relate them to vastly different and often severely discrepant world of meaning and experience. Modern life is typically segmented to a very high degree, and it is important to understand that this segmentation (or, as we prefer to call it, pluralization) is not only manifest on the level of observable social conduct but also has important manifestations on the level of consciousness (Berger

et.al., 1979:62–63).

It can also be said that modernity gives us the choice: the freedom to select from diverse possibilities. It is in this context that I wish to look at my own process of growing up. I see this 'modern' experience while shifting from a small town to a big city. In a city I see an entirely new world filled with immense possibilities. I see experimentations all around. I see a Satyajit Ray film, a painting exhibition in the art gallery, I listen to an experimental singer, know about innumerable professions and vocations, and find diverse groups working in the field of environment, gender, health and education. In other words, the city as a modern site makes things happen, allows me to come out of a small, protected, closed network, and cultivate what Lerner would have regarded as the 'empathy of the mobile personality': the capacity to incorporate new demands upon oneself, or to see oneself in the other fellow's situation (Lerner, 2000: 121–23). It is in this sense that modernity expands one's horizon, and perpetually transforms the world around us. This heightened 'psychic mobility' is something that I know I would miss if I am asked to live in, say, an insulated village where, as it would be argued, nothing happens except the recurrence of routinized everyday life-practices.

The inherent dynamism of modernity implies the process of *individuation*: individuals can rediscover themselves, unfold their potential, and evolve their own life-projects. Nothing can be imposed on them simply because of their birth in a caste, clan or community. One is not born with one's destiny; one makes it. In other words, modernity means a radical shift: from fatalism to active agency, from ascription to achievement, from passivity to meaningful choice. No wonder, Alex Inkels—a high priest of modernity—would regard the abandonment of passivity and fatalism, and 'the assertion of increasing independence from the authority of traditional figures like parents and priests as the major characteristic of a modern man (Inkels,

2000:134–43). This means that as individuals endowed with agency we can now choose. My father may be a Brahmin scholar, but I can choose to join a management school, and start my own business. Or, I may be born in a lower caste family in Uttar Pradesh, but I can become the chief minister of the state. The arousal of this active agency, it has to be realized, is indeed a great strength of modernity. It gives confidence, particularly to the victims of a traditional social order, to rediscover their own possibilities, and create a new world free from the burden of *karma*, fatalism and ascriptive status. It is, however, true that the individual cannot be seen in isolation. We know that the liberal ethos of modernity asserts the agency of the individual. As Max Weber would have said, man is a conscious agent capable of attaching his own meaning to the world. But then, there were sociologists who thought somewhat differently. Individualism, for Emile Durkheim, should not be equated with the utilitarian notion of man as a discrete individual concerned only with the maximization of his own pleasure. Durkheim's individual could not be altogether free from the overwhelming power of the collective. And Karl Marx took class, not bourgeois individualism as the unit of analysis. Yet, neither Durkheim nor Marx—because of their affinity with the core spirit of modernity—could deny the liberating role of human agency. Durkheim saw and celebrated differentiation and specialization in modern societies. And Marx would have felt happy had he seen that many socio-political movements in our times—from the lower caste movement to the feminist assertion—have been inspired by this modernist belief that we are not puppets, and we can create our own histories. Not solely that. This freedom to choose in a pluralistic universe, it is said, is truly rational. Because the new form of division of labour, it is believed, allows individuals to opt for appropriate vocations that suit their specific aptitudes. Even if my father is a Brahmin priest, I have no particular obligation to choose my father's vocation, if I am not inclined to it. I may join a film institute, and become a film maker. The argument is that this division of labour which is rooted in the process of inviduation taps the best in each of us. The modern age, therefore, becomes more rational, efficient and productive.

The process of individuation—or the arousal of agency—means that modernity leads to the *democratization* of society. It intends to free the individual from the tyranny of caste, clan and religion. Not solely that. As an individual one becomes important—a being to be respected in one's own right. In fact, many major movements in modern (particularly Western) thought and culture contributed to the emergence of this new conception. The Reformation and Protestantism set the individual conscience free from the religious institutions of the Church and exposed it directly to the eye of God; Renaissance humanism placed man at the centre of the universe; the scientific revolutions endowed man with the capacity to enquire into the mysteries of nature, and the Enlightenment, centred on the image of rational, scientific man, created a social milieu free from dogma and intolerance. Indeed, the birth of the individual as a political subject is a distinctive feature of modernity. He has *rights* as an individual, and these rights cannot be abolished in the name of some communitarian identity, even if communities have their relative autonomy. Democracy must rest on the individual, his autonomy and rights. The various Declarations and Bills of Rights of the American Revolution, the *Declaration des Droits de L'Homme* of the French Revolution, and similar statements in country after country, until the eventual adoption of supranational declarations by the United Nations (1948) became an almost inevitable ingredient of the modern political discourse. Yes, modernity—its primary importance to the individual and his/her rights—makes democracy an integral component of political culture. Political democracy, it would not be wrong to say, is often seen as a hallmark of modernity. And we do experience tremendous gains of this political culture. Democracy means freedom, transparency, openness, the ability to dissent, and the willingness to listen to others. Democracy means that everyone, black or white, rich or poor, has his space, and it has to be respected. As a matter of fact, modernity, because of its democratic spirit, creates a culture of debate, dissent and refutation. The ban on this intellectual and artistic/aesthetic freedom is seen as sort of pre-modern/medieval orthodoxy.

Yes, modernity gives birth to the 'autonomous' individual. His/her 'private' domain is protected and respected. In other words, modernity—because of its rational/liberal ethos—is likely to abhor the idea of undue interference in one's private life. Yet, this affirmation of an autonomous individual does by no means suggest that there is no shared public space in which private individuals can come, meet, communicate, and work together. Instead, modernity, it is asserted by its adherents, promotes an entire matrix of *civil society*—media, educational/cultural institutions and voluntary associations—in which people communicate, articulate their voices, and tend to create a shared inter-subjective world. Between an autonomous individual and the state lies all sorts of intermediate institutions. And the vibrancy of a modern society depends on this entire network of civil society. In fact, there are proponents of modernity who would argue that it is important to preserve and strengthen this shared public space. Because if the individual becomes isolated, and the state adopts manipulative strategies, modernity would degenerate into an 'iron cage', it would lose its humanness, and its open/dialogic character. A vibrant public sphere in which individuals are engaged in free communication would distinguish a truly modern society from an orthodox/closed system. I guess Habermas was hinting precisely at this possibility when he celebrated the ideal of the *public sphere*:

> By the public sphere we mean first of all a realm of our social life in which something approaching public opinion can be formed... Citizens behave as a public body when they confer in an unrestricted fashion—that is, with the guarantee of freedom of assembly and association and the freedom to express and publish their opinions—about matters of general interest. . . the expression 'public opinion' refers to the tasks of criticism and control which a public body of citizens informally practises...vis-a-vis a ruling class (Quoted in Pusey, 1987:89).

In other words, the vibrant public sphere can well be a site of what Habermas would regard as 'communicative rationality' leading to a social milieu filled with reciprocity, symmetry and the ethos of understanding. Well, Habermas is deeply aware of the fact that late capitalism often distorts the possibility of free communication, because it manipulates the public opinion through the mass media, or the forced articulation of social needs through large organizations. But then, the answer, for Habermas, lies not in an escape from modernity. The answer is to unfold the very potential of modernity. He reminds us of this potential, and pleads for a reconstructed rationality in which reason becomes active in politics and history through the free interpretation, in an unrestricted social interaction, of the issues, events and interests that govern our destiny. In other words, modernity does not mean well-fed/well-clothed individuals—politically indifferent and culturally insensitive—living in their own little worlds. As Habermas reminds us, it should mean a vibrant public sphere in which people participate and reflect on the world.

Even the most enthusiastic adherents of modernity admit that these ideals—critical consciousness, respect to the autonomy of the individual, and open/democratic public culture—are not always easy to practise. Instead, as we have seen, many societies which are otherwise modern (industrial, technologically-developed and urbanized) have betrayed the spirit of democracy; the gains of modernity have been monopolized by the select few, not necessarily distributed amongst all. In other words, oppression, inequality and authoritarianism have not altogether disappeared from the modern world. Who can, for instance, forget that in the twentieth century the 'modern' West experienced the worst from of authoritarianism, and brutality of war and violence? This despair could indeed be seen in Max Weber's anguish over the 'disenchantment' of the world, in Sigmund Freud's powerful articulations of the 'discontents' of civilization, in the 'dialectic' of Enlightenment Adorno and Horkheimer talked about, in the existentialist preoccupation with 'death' and 'nothingness', and possibly in the mood of 'deconstruction' in which contemporary postmodernists indulge themselves. But then, what is distinctive about modernity, as its proponents argue, is that it can evolve its own critique; it is self-reflexive; it is capable of finding a solution within the discourse of modernity itself. Modernity, it is argued, is essentially optimistic in nature. Take, for instance, what is broadly known as Marxism. Yes, Marx was modern: a child of Enlightenment, a rational thinker who believed in science, and its ability to overcome ideological distortions, and illuminate us with the light of 'true consciousness'. He cherished the dynamism in history: the way it evolves itself, assumes a linear path, and moves towards 'progress'. But then, Marx's modernity was not in tune with what he was experiencing in his own time: the capitalist social order filled with commodity fetishism, private property, exploitation of the working class, and alienated labour. Yes, capitalism, Marx argued, was a breakthrough; it was a product of industrial revolution, an assertion of the emergent bourgeoisie, and a necessary stage towards historical progress.

> The bourgeoisie, by the rapid improvement of all instruments of production, by the immensely facilitated means of communication, draws all, even the most barbarian nations into civilization. . . It has created enormous cities, has increased the urban population as compared with the rural, and has thus rescued a considerable part of the population from the idiocy of rural life. . . It has made barbarian and semi-barbarian countries dependent on the civilized ones, nations of peasants on nations of bourgeoisie, the East on the West (Marx and Engels, 1975: 47–48).

Yet, the progressive/modernist role the bourgeoisie played, for Marx, was incomplete and contradictory. Because this modernity, he thought, values only callous 'cash payment'.

> It has resolved personal worth into exchange value, and in place of the numberless indefeasible chartered freedoms, has set up that single, unconscionable freedom—Free Trade. In one word, for exploitation, veiled by religious and political illusions, it has substituted naked, shameless, direct, brutal exploitation (Ibid: 44–45).

No wonder, for the Marxists, capitalism cannot become people's modernity or emancipatory modernity. Yet, this critique does by no means suggest that Marx was cherishing a nostalgia for a 'non-modern' world. Instead, as we have already said, he was a passionate believer in modernity, its rationality and scientificity. He was, therefore, suggesting what his followers would regard as a more mature, fulfilling, affirmative modernity: a socialist/communist society free from the fragmented/exploited character of capitalism.

What we are noticing is, therefore, interesting. For the Marxists, the answer to capitalism—even when 'it has drowned the most heavenly ecstasies of religious fervour, of chivalrous enthusiasm, of philistine sentimentalism, in the icy water of egotistical calculation' (Ibid: 44)—lies in modernity itself, not in a regressive journey to the 'golden' past. And for Habermas, unlike his predecessors Adorno and Marcuse, even when late capitalism leads to 'the colonization of the life-world', the answer is not to grow cynical about modernity, but to accomplish its unfinished agenda. As a matter of fact, what we are seeing is some kind of a balanced optimism in modernity. Modernity has its problems, but it is capable of finding a reasonable solution. I wish to recall an example from Anthony Giddens. Giddens is careful enough to reveal the crisis of modernity—its possible 'risks' (Giddens, 1990). For instance, in modern times the surveillance capabilities of the state and capitalist enterprise have increased dramatically; there is indeed the increased risk of the growth of totalitarian power. Likewise, the second risk is associated with the 'industrialization of war'. And the third risk is about the potential collapse of economic growth systems. Finally, there is yet another risk that involves the potential for ecological disaster. But then, what is interesting is that Giddens does not succumb to pessimism. He sees immense possibilities in various social movements. The labour movement seeks to address the risk tendencies of capitalism, whereas democratic movements challenge authoritarianism, peace movements challenge militarization, and ecological movements seek to remedy threats to the global environment. In other words, the proponents of modernity want to convince us that it is capable of innovating itself, and it is in a perpetual process of exploration and experimentation. I feel that Giddens is taking about the same thing when he asserts that 'the reflexivity of modern social life consists in the fact that social practices are constantly examined and reformed in the light of incoming information about these very practices, thus constitutively altering their character' (Ibid: 38).

These values—freedom, criticality, democratization,

openness and optimism for the future—seem to have become desirable ideals/guidelines for the entire human kind. Irrespective of cultural differences, it is difficult to legitimate a civilization that does not adore these values. It is in this sense that one can argue that modernity is irreversible, and even if you and I have our distinctive projects of modernity, we cannot deny this critical minimum. Take, for instance, our own specific Indian modernity. It is possible to argue that here caste—not liberal individualism—is the governing principle. Yet, as our Constitution acknowledges, the rights of the individual are no less important. Likewise, even if the 'personal' laws of a religious community have their space, it is becoming increasingly difficult to support patriarchal hierarchy and oppression. In other words, no society that seeks to call itself modern can escape the moral pressure of these core values.

But then, there is a complex dialectic that needs to be acknowledged. It is not necessarily right to say that modernity was something that happened only at a specific juncture of history (eighteenth-century Enlightenment) in a specific geographical locality (Europe). True, the Enlightenment agenda with its Kant, Voltaire and Montesquie, and subsequent politico-economic changes in the world ranging from the Industrial Revolution to the French Revolution helped consolidating the roots of modernity. But then, even in the past, in tradition, or in 'non-modern' periods one can notice the traces of the core values of modernity which we are talking about. It is in this sense that the dichotomy of modernity and tradition, or modern and non-modern becomes problematic. Look at our own tradition. Even for a vehement critic, it is not difficult to see that our tradition has a space for the culture of criticality and dissent. Each time I read the *Upanishads*, I get inspired by the critical/dialogic spirit that these discourses create. For example, the great philosophic argumentation and contestation that characterize the conversation between Yajnavalkya and Gargi in the *Brhad-aranayak-Upanishad* is immensely illuminating (B.U.III8.1–III 8.12). Likewise, the dissenting voices can be seen in Buddhism and Jainism, or in bhakti/sufi traditions. The question, therefore arises: was Yajnavalkya or Buddha modern or traditional? As matter of fact, we often realize the limitations of these categories. Possibly the only thing we can talk about is that the core values of modernity are not necessarily always Euro-centric. Modernity can also be experienced as a continuity with tradition. We see this continuity in many finer Indian minds. Tagore, for instance, could reconcile his inclination to the *Upanishadic* prayer with his openness to modern scientific ideas. And Gandhi, despite being a 'santani Hindu', could lead modern political movements. It is, therefore, important not to see modernity as something necessarily 'alien' coming from the West. It is also important not to see tradition as merely a site of superstitions and prejudices. As a matter of fact, such a rigid dichotomy can have disastrous political implications. Every student of sociology knows that the theory of modernity that emerged in the post-war era often legitimated the American hegemony, and produced stereotypes about 'non-modern' cultures. Yes, as I myself have stated, there are positive insights that we can indeed learn from the modernists like Lerner and Inkels. But then, we must be careful about their political implications. If not used creatively, these discourses would reproduce stereotypes about other cultures.

Having said this, I must also add that we should not underestimate the historic role of the Enlightenment in the making of modernity. Yes, there was a culture of debate and openness in the *Upanishads*, there was a fairly developed system of logic and reasoning in our philosophies like *Nayaya* and *Mimamsa*, and there was Kabir/Nanak interrogating the culture of orthodoxy. But the larger society as a whole could not necessarily universalize and institutionalize these core values. It was only in modern times (and we have to acknowledge the historic contributions of the European Enlightenment) that these values, far from being limited to select saints, mystics and learned castes, would be a collective aspiration, and get institutionalized through a network of new institutions and structures like liberal democracy and a vibrant civil society. In other words, even though there is a continuity between tradition and modernity, there is a distinctive character of modernity in terms of politico-economic and cultural institutions which have legitimated these core values. And, despite my many critiques of modernity, I believe that these values, if lived in an immensely delicate and creative fashion, can indeed enrich our life.

II
The Other Side of Modernity: Burden of Arrogance

It is, however, important to realize that modernity is a double-edged phenomenon. While its core values have a liberating potential, its concrete practices may cause arrogance and violence. It is like being excessively proud of oneself, and looking at others with a sense of contempt. I am rational, modern, and enlightened; you are ignorant, superstitious and barbaric! It is like dividing and hierarchizing the world. If we look at history, we notice this arrogance of modernity—particularly, the hyper-modernity of the West.

The fact is that here is a project that is terribly proud of itself. This sense of pride lies in its immense achievements and promises. To be part of the modernizing process, one is often led to believe, is like celebrating a new world: something that is radically different from all that happened earlier. It creates a world that seems to resemble the design of a perfect rational order. The Kingdom of Reason, it is hoped, is filled with freedom, prosperity and comfort. Possibly the techno-industrial culture that modernity brings with it makes it possible. The modern age, unlike all other periods, knows the science of controlling and tapping natural resources, and utilizes these resources for the material well-being of the human species. Not solely that. It knows the technology of mass production. As a result, it is only in the modern period that everyone—at least potentially—is capable of enjoying the fruits of the ever-expanding comfort industry. And for the first time in human history, it is possible for man to be free from the necessities, and enter the domain of freedom. Indeed, Marx could imagine his *whole man*—a man cultivating all the faculties of his being—only in the modern age. Because science is power, and technology promises to rescue man from routinized and time-consuming manual labour. It does things with efficiency and speed, and gives comfort to man. Each new technological discovery speaks of its promise, its almost miraculous power, and seduces man. Technologies become more and more sophisticated, efficient and user-friendly. From computer to mobile phone, from video camera to washing machine, from MRI scan to latest medical gadget—everywhere one hears the same story: the way technologies make life smooth, easy and comfortable. The more modern we are the more surrounded we are with technologies. The more modern we are the more rational/smooth/efficient we are. It is this difference—the ability to do things much faster and more efficiently—that strikes one immediately when one migrates to a 'developed' country (say, the USA) from a 'developing' country (say India). These technological comforts that modernity provides declare their own success stories. No wonder, self-advertisement becomes an inseparable component of the age of modernity. It is proud of itself, it is certain in its achievements, and it knows that it is capable of seducing people. It is, therefore, not surprising that in this proud/

modern world we experience the all-pervasive culture of ads. Everything around us is filled with ads: narratives, beliefs, hopes and images of success—success of divergent brands of detergent, car, school, hospital... In such a world Vance Packard is not entirely wrong when he says that 'we no longer buy oranges, we buy vitality; we do not buy just an auto, we buy prestige' (Packard, 1982:15). Yes, modernity makes us believe that nothing is impossible. It exaggerates its achievements, and mythologizes its success. Its proud discourse of development attaches a stigmatized identity to 'underdeveloped' nations.

There is yet another reason why so much pride is associated with this brand of modernity. Look at its self-awareness. It assumes that it is capable of generating the foundation of objective, rational and universal knowledge. In other words, the ability to decipher such a foundation, it was hoped, would distinguish the period of modernity from all other periods when men supposedly lived under diverse irrational/mystical religious beliefs, blind social customs, and obscurantist practices. This new knowledge, it was believed, would bring enlightenment, overcome darkness, and enable us to understand, control and shape our destinies. Not surprisingly, modernity became triumphant through its scientific knowledge. All 'non-scientific' knowledges were getting marginalized. Because modernity divided the world into dualistic opposites: Baconian empiricism vs. 'idols' filled with sentiments and prejudices; Cartesian disembodied rationality vs. emotive/bodily sensations and feelings, and science vs. metaphysics. Science with its Newton and Darwin became the most privileged/legitimate knowledge—not just about the physical world, but also about the socio-cultural world. History was distinguished from mythology, and sociology from philosophy. This pride in science as objective/foundational knowledge became rather manifest in what is known as *positivism*: the belief that it is only through a 'scientific' way of understanding that we can create a new rational world. This pride manifested itself in all modern institutions: universities must teach modern knowledges, not mythology, theology or cosmology; hospitals must cultivate 'modern' medicine, not traditional forms of healing; and institutions must be governed by 'rational' bureaucracies, not traditional/charismatic forms of authority.

> The assumption of the inherent superiority of science has moved beyond science and has become an article of faith for almost everyone...Human relations are subjected to scientific treatment as is shown by education programmes, proposals for prison reform, army training and so on. The power of medical profession over every stage of our lives already exceeds the power once wielded by the Church. Almost all scientific subjects are compulsory on our schools. While the parents of a six year old can decide to have him instructed in the rudiments of Protestantism, or in the rudiments of Jewish faith, or to other religious instruction altogether, they do not have similar freedom in the case of sciences. Physics, astronomy, history must be learned: they cannot be replaced by magic, astrology, or by a study of legends (Feyerabend, 1978:74).

Indeed, to be modern, it is felt, is to be superior, because one is blessed with scientific knowledge. And because of this pride, Paul Feyerabend is bold enough to reveal that 'the apostles of science acted like 'determined conquerors; they materially suppressed the bearers of all alternative traditions' (Ibid: 102). I can understand Feyerabend's anguish. The modern age defined itself as the age of Reason, and it led to a series of binary oppositions: science against religion and magic, truth against prejudice, and rationality against the rule of custom. No wonder, from the vantage point of modernity, all other forms of life were seen as pathological, a residue of the past—something to be overcome. Feyerabend, who pleaded for the plurality of methods, needless to add, could not give his consent to the hegemony of modern scientism.

Furthermore, scientific rationalism tends to generate the fetish of 'objectivity' that deviates man from himself and turns the act of scientific knowledge into an act of alienation. This possibly explains the capacity of human beings to turn on their environment and their fellows with 'the cool and meticulously calculated rapacity of industrial society' (Roszak, 1972: 168). Environmental disaster, it has to be realized, is an inevitable outcome of this sort of scientism which has no sense of humility, wonder and enchantment, and reduces nature into a 'resource'—something to be measured and quantified in terms of the principles of positivistic economics. In fact, it is not just violence against nature out there; it is violence itself: a doctrine of war. I think that it is this criticality that has also led J.P.S. Uberoi to see the devastating Manhattan Project as an expression of the 'science of vivisection' (Uberoi, 2002:82–101).

> Everything is alive in dualistic parts and nothing is whole in this civilization any longer: truth and reality, the good and the bad, life and death, knowledge or contemplation and action, the spirit and the form. God is dead to the world of course, but the human species and the science of nature do not look so good either—at any rate to the non-expert and the non-elite: God is dead, and I am not feeling too well either! (Ibid: 90).

It is at this juncture that I must remind the readers that I am not jumping into the cult of irrationality. I do not belong to a camp that calls itself 'anti-science'. But then, I must say that the arrogance of science must be resisted. Science and science alone can take us to the domain of truth—this cognitive power of science also becomes its political power. Not surprisingly, science often becomes an ideology of the modern nation-state. From scientific management to scientific socialism to scientific development—the dominant ideologies seek to marginalize all alternative voices. If the state manufactures nuclear weapons, it is seen as a development of science. Or, for that matter, if Medha Patkar protests against big dams, it is seen as anti-development and hence anti-science. And the irony is that even some of the alternative voices, in order to prove their legitimacy, begin to appropriate the language of science. Modern godmen quote quantum mechanics, and prove the 'science' of the Vedanta, and traditional healing practices like yoga and ayurveda become 'modern', and appeal to the 'scientific' community. This does not mean that science has to be eradicated, and relativism established. Instead, what is important to realize is that there is a huge domain of uncertainty, and objective/deterministic science alone is inadequate to make sense of the world. It is important to create a world in which a scientist and a mystic, an engineer and a poet, a modern physician and a traditional healer co-exist, and enrich one another. Because, as Uberoi would argue, 'truth emerges from the dialectics of what is the case (present) and what is not the case (absent), the world of reality and the still wider world of possibility' (Ibid: 91). What is sad is that, despite radical changes in the philosophy of science, many of us continue to think in the positivistic mode. As a result, science becomes arrogant; science legitimates the practice of social engineering done by the techno-managerial elite.

As a matter of fact, this certainty implicit in modernity—its self-pride, its assertion that it leads to prosperity and happiness, and its belief that it is based on foundational knowledge—has made it into a terribly arrogant endeavour. Its self-awareness as a superior project has indeed hierarchized cultures and civilizations. Historically we have seen how the modern West—the centre of modernity—distinguished itself from other 'non-modern' (or non-

Western) civilizations: how it constructed the notion of the Orient, its backwardness, and its striking isolation from the mainstream of European progresses in science, arts and commerce (Said, 1973). Even an emancipatory thinker like Karl Marx, as we are realizing with pain and astonishment, could not escape this modernist/Euro-centric pride. For Marx, England, despite the crimes she made in India, played a 'regenerating' role; she abolished the foundation of 'Oriental despotism', she was the unconscious tool of history, and brought India to the 'mainstream' civilization (Quoted in Said, 1973:153). Yes, Edward Said's path-breaking work, I would argue, has sensitized us. We can now see the arrogance of the modernist project—how Orientalism sustains itself by making authorizing statements about the Orient: 'its eccentricity, its backwardness, its silent indifference, its feminine penetrability, its supine malleability' (Ibid: 206). Orientalism, for Said, exists as 'a Western style for dominating, restructuring, and having authority over the orient' (Ibid: 3). The hierarchy of cultures and the superiority of Western modernity became obvious because the Orient was seen as 'a locale requiring Western attention, reconstruction, and even redemption'. (Ibid: 206).

This self-awareness of Western modernity as a 'superior' project, as we are realizing, made it inseparable from the history of colonialism. Because what was distinctive about colonialism was that it often legitimated itself through its 'civilizing' mission. It asserted that it had introduced reason, science, industry and school; in other words, it illuminated and rescued the colonized from the domain of darkness. A society like ours did experience the arrogance of this sort of colonial modernity. Recall the discourse of modern/English education that Thomas Babington Macaulay introduced in India. He refused to acknowledge anything worth preserving in the Indic civilization. For him, 'a single shelf of a good European library was worth the whole native literature of India and Arabia' (Quoted in Pathak, 2002: 79). With his characteristic arrogance (and this arrogance emanated from a belief that the West has already reached the ultimate stage of secular salvation) and the resultant feeling of charity, he argued that only through new modern education could the British save this 'decadent' civilization.

> ...What is power worth if it is founded on vice, on ignorance, and on misery, if we can hold it only by violating the most sacred duties which as governors, we owe to the governed, and which, as people blessed with far more than ordinary measure of political liberty and of intellectual light, we owe to a race debased by three thousand years of despotism and priest craft? We are free, we are civilized to little purpose if we grudge to any portion of the human race an equal measure of freedom and civilization (Ibid: 79).

What we notice in this colonial modernity is that it demoralizes the colonized; it assumes that the colonized have yet to become rational, adult, masculine and civilized, and they need to be taught the lessons of modernity by the colonial masters. It is therefore, no wonder that colonialism, as Ashis Nandy has argued with a remarkable insight, sanctifies a worldview that privileges 'the absolute superiority of the human over the nonhuman and the subhuman, the masculine over the feminine, the adult over the child, the historical over the ahistorical, and the modern or progressive over the traditional or the savage' (Nandy, 1983:X). In this process, Nandy adds, 'it helps generalize the concept of the modern West from a geographical and temporal entity to a psychological category (Ibid: XI). As a result, the colonized tend to lose faith in themselves. They seek to redefine themselves through colonial categories.

> In the colonial culture, identification with the aggressor bound the rulers and the ruled in an unbreakable dyadic relationship. The Raj saw Indians as crypto barbarians

> who needed to further civilize themselves. It saw British rule as an agent of progress and as a mission. Many Indians in turn saw their salvation in becoming more like the British, in friendship or in enemy. (Ibid: 7).

We are now realizing that a significant section of the new elite that was born of colonial modernity in India sought to reaffirm the same worldview. Even a Marxist historian like Sumit Sarkar who, unlike recent theorists of postmodernism, believed in the virtues of Enlightenment, could not fail to problematize the early modernists in India. For example, as he argued, it is important to be aware of the fact that Rammohun and his generation ardently welcomed 'the negative, alienating aspects of the English education' (Sarkar, 1985: 8). This Renaissance culture, Sarkar believes, entertained an illusion: a long continued faith in basic British good intentions (Ibid: 68). That was indeed the tragedy. Modern colonialism, as Nandy would argue, won its great victories not so much through its military and technological power as through the agenda of modernity: the ideologies of progress, normality and hyper-masculinity, and in theories of cumulative growth of science and technology. That was why, even some of the finest critical minds in India felt that 'colonialism, by introducing modern structures into the barbaric world, would open up the non-West to the modern critical—analytic spirit' (Nandy, 1983: ix).

This arrogance, let it be stated, does by no means suggest that there are no gains of modernity. Modernity, I have already stated, has immense gains and achievements. Furthermore, it is equally important to become humble on our part, acknowledge our shortcomings, and see modernity also as a positive reference point. As I feel, it is desirable to think of a truly cross-cultural dialogue, and a spirit of humility and openness, rather than a closed/arrogant mind-set. It is like asserting the need for a two-way process: *(a)* modern West willing to learn from non-Western traditions in order to correct itself, and *(b)* we begin to appreciate the core values of modernity in order to create a better world. Let the modern West become humble, and learn that India, despite innumerable problems, didn't live in a dark age as Macaulay imagined. Here is an old/vibrant civilization sustained by rich philosophic traditions, splendid diversity in cultural practices, and a spirit of syncreticism. Let its Max Webers learn that our religions are not necessarily 'other-worldly'; instead, the ideal of the unity of the material and the spiritual, the sacred and the profane have sought to give a distinctively positive meaning to life which, as Sudhir Kakar showed with a remarkably brilliant insight, produces 'not the Oedipuses and the Hamlets but the Nachiketas and the Meeras', (Kakar, 1981: 29). But then, it is equally important on our part to acknowledge that we have to overcome many of our fatalistic beliefs and oppressive social practices, and we do not belittle ourselves if we learn from Voltaire and Kant, and if we see something positive that has taken place in the post-Enlightenment West. This mutual learning, or the 'fusion of horizons', I believe, ought to characterize an open world we are striving for. It is, therefore, debatable whether the theorists of postmodernity—the way they relativize cultures, suspect the Enlightenment belief in progress, and delegitimize science as 'foundational knowledge'—necessarily offer a meaningful/sustainable alternative to modernity. However, I wish to argue, it is nevertheless desirable to grow humble; it is better to learn from those who are 'non-modern', who are not like 'us'. Modernity can humanize itself if it is engaged in 'the art of civilized conversation'. I give my consent to Zygmunt Bauman when he pleads for humble 'interpreters' of multiple cultural traditions, and the need 'to talk to people rather than fight them; to understand them rather than dismiss or annihilate them as mutants; to enhance one's own tradition by drawing freely on experience from other pools, rather than shutting it off from the traffic of ideas'. (Bauman, 1987:143)

III
Existential Anguish and Unhappy Consciousness

Modernity has also its history of pain, anguish and suffering. The promise of modernity, we have been repeatedly told, is its spirit of freedom. Yet, how often we experience that not everything about the modern world is necessarily always about freedom. Modernity, it should not be forgotten, needs massive structures—techno-industrial enterprises, legal systems and educational machineries which, because of their very nature, are complex, and require expertised knowledge, and, therefore, get increasingly mystified. No wonder, these very institutions which are expected to preserve our modern rights tend to become alienating. The spirit of freedom is lost amidst the huge machinery, and its technicality. Indeed, it is not at all impossible to experience the constraints of bureaucratic/technocratic rules and disciplinary regimes all around. We begin to realize that we are not as free as we are asked to believe. As a matter of fact, there is often a pressure to submit to what 'experts' and 'specialists' regard as 'normal' and 'desirable'. We realize the politics of knowledge: how knowledge and power are integrally linked, how 'experts', 'specialists', or, to use Foucault's words, 'normalizing judges' are perpetually observing, disciplining and hierarchizing us. Take, for instance, the assertion of Reason: rational/objective/scientific knowledge. All modern institutions—hospitals, schools and courts—seek to protect this discourse, and exercise a power over those they supervise, train and correct, 'over madmen, children at home and at school, the colonized, over those who are stuck at a machine and supervised for the rest of their lives' (Foucault, 1982: 29). Because the individual in the disciplinary regime has to be 'described, judged, measured and compared with others;

he has to be 'trained or corrected, classified, normalized, excluded etc' (Ibid: 191). If I do not follow 'reason', I am mad, and it is the task of a psychiatrist to control my 'irrationality' so that I can assume 'normality'. If I do not go to school, and do not learn its 'expertized' knowledge and curriculum, I am not 'educated'. In other words, I need to be 'rational', 'educated', 'healthy' and 'normal'—everything as defined by experts, institutions and knowledge-systems. I, therefore, get thoroughly 'disciplined'. My body, my education, my morals and even my death—everything is defined, measured, recorded and decided by the 'experts' in this 'disciplinary regime' or the 'administered totality'.

It is in this context that I wish to recall the death of a dear one in our family. One morning she passed away. It was a peaceful death. Her face revealed the beauty of her last journey. But then, I could not really contemplate, and make sense of this death because I was reminded by a friend of mine that a doctor had to be called immediately. A doctor—and a doctor alone—with his 'expertized' knowledge could 'declare' her dead. And this death certificate, I was told, I must carry with me while taking her to the cremation ground. I must 'register' her death. In other words, I realized that there was no escape from the 'expertized gaze' even at the ultimate moment of death. Yes, that day I realized why Michel Foucault did talk about 'surveillance' in our times, the way the disciplinary regime situates individuals in 'a network of writing', and 'engages them in a whole mass of documents that capture and fix them'. (Ibid: 189). The point I am trying to state is that the age of modernity, despite its grand promise of freedom, has its own story of surveillance. Possibly this control mechanism has become more subtle, more refined, or more 'scientific'. That is why, I recall Foucault's *Discipline and Punish,* and appreciate the point he made. For example, if we think of penalty or punishment in the new age, the physical torture of the body 'as a public spectacle' is no longer important. Instead, the 'experts' with new knowledges emerge, and begin to 'discipline' us. And this process, needless to add, is now more sophisticated and technically designed.

> A whole army of technicians took over from the executioner, the immediate antagonist of pain: wardens, doctors, chaplains, psychiatrists, psychologists, educationalists; by their very presence near the prisoner, they sing the praises that the law needs: they reassure it that the body and pain are not the ultimate objects of its punitive action. Today a doctor must watch over those condemned to death, right up to the last moment—thus juxtaposing himself as the agent of welfare, as the alleviator of pain, with the official whose task it is to end life. This is worth thinking about. When the moment of execution approaches, the patients are injected with tranquilizers. A utopia of judicial reticence: take away life, but prevent the patient from feeling it; deprive the prisoner of all rights, but do not inflict pain; impose penalties free of all pain... (Ibid: 11).

Doubtless, in the modern age I am 'free' in the sense that I can vote, choose my representative, and buy any commodity I like from the shopping mall. But then, there is another aspect of my being that is being perpetually observed, measured, compared, documented, and controlled. This disciplinary power, Foucault reminded us, is 'calculated, organized and technically thought out'. (Ibid: 26). Time and again we hear the recurrence of this warning: modernity brings with it heavy structures which, because of their very nature, are alienating. Weber saw it as an 'iron cage'. Kafka's novels revealed man's utter helplessness before a huge bureaucratic machinery, critical theorists saw the all-pervasive domination in the techno-scientific apparatus, Illich saw the denial of human freedom in schools and hospitals, and Foucault spoke of 'the revolts against model prisons, tranquilizers, isolation, the medical or educational services' (Ibid: 30). It is important to be aware of this darker aspect of modernity. But then, it would be naive to romanticize a 'non-modern' world which, everyone knows, had its own principle of oppression. As we look at our own culture, we could notice these oppressive practices: how, say, the tyranny of caste structures denied man's creativity and agency which possibly led a dissenter like Jyotiba Phule to express his anguish over institutionalized Hinduism by arguing that in his ideal family there would be no scope for a Hindu, whereas the father would be a Buddhist, the mother a Christian, the daughter a Muslim and the son a *satya dharmist*. It is, therefore, important to be cautious. The critique of modernity should not be allowed to be hijacked by the revivalists trying to sanctify the 'golden' past. I am suggesting something far deeper. I am arguing that we must rescue modernity from being degenerated into an oppressive/disciplinary regime. We do not want just the scientific efficiency of the machine, or the instrumental rationality of the market. We also need the poetry of life. We need to soften modernity. It is in this context that I wish to recall a great lesson that I have learned from *romanticism*. It defied the worship of Reason, pleaded for the intensity of imagination and creativity, and man's right to deviate from the 'normal' and 'everyday'. It sought to open our eyes, and make us experience the world like enchanted seers, and feel its magic, wonder and beauty that transcend the cold logic of science.

> *Sweet is the lore which Nature brings,*
> *Our meddling intellect*
> *Mis-shapes the beauteous forms of things:*
> *We murder to dissect*
>
> (Quoted in Bloom and Trilling, 1973:129).

The poetry of William Wordsworth is indeed a reminder. Not everyone can remain contented with modernity: its reason, its scientificity, and its technicality. Well, it is possible to argue that the anguish/pain/suffering we are talking about has been exaggerated; it is just a small price one has to pay for achieving the enormous gains of modernity. The adherents of modernity might ask: isn't it true that modernity, precisely because of its science and disciplinary devices, has enabled us to experience increased longevity, better health awareness, improved literacy and tremendous comfort? Yes, it is indeed true. But then, there is yet another aspect of our being which neither a rationalist nor a technogist understands. Possibly it requires a poet, a mystic, a mad man who make us strive for the heightened imagination—the ecstasy of the transcendental dance, or the willingness to lead a life which, even if not 'rational', is immensely fulfilling and meaningful. I think there is much to learn—even today—from the way Shelley defended poetry way back in the early nineteenth century:

> We want the creative faculty to imagine that which we know; we want the generous impulse to act that which we imagine; we want the poetry of life: our calculations have outrun conception; we have eaten more than we can digest. The cultivation of those sciences which have enlarged the limits of the empire of man over the external world, has, for want of poetical faculty, proportionally circumscribed those of the internal world; and man, having enslaved the elements, remains himself a slave. To what but a cultivation of the mechanical arts in a degree disproportioned to the presence of the creative faculty, which is the basis of all knowledge, is to be attributed for abridging and combining labour, to the exasperation of the inequality of mankind? From what other cause has it arisen that these inventions which should have lightened, have added a weight to the curse imposed on Adam? Thus poetry, and the principle of self, of which money is the visible incarnation, are the God and Mammon of the world. (Quoted in Bloom and

Trilling, 1973: 757).

Here is yet another story of suffering—not physical suffering, but the deeper suffering of the soul. See the immense mobility that modernity generates. Its railway stations, its airports, and its express highways do indicate the dynamism of modernity: people are moving and moving for better prospects: for jobs, health, commerce and education. There is restlessness all around: a continual search for something more, something better. Yes, this mobility has its own narratives of achievement—say, a girl from a remote village in Bihar coming to Delhi to get education and livelihood, and thereby altering her life-project, or a boy from Kerala leaving the ancestral village for finding a better prospect in Dubai. Needless to add, these new opportunities elevate the economy, and the mode of living. Yet, beneath these opportunities lies the experience of heightened loneliness. With increasing mobility and migration one tends to lose the living contact with one's parents, siblings, one's community, and the cultural/ physical landscape in which one is born. This often leads to the existential anguish called 'homelessness'. There are many who cannot escape this sadness: the sadness born out of the ambiguity inherent in the modernizing process. It gives you comfort, career and opportunities; yet, it deprives you of unconditional intimacy. Because of the 'migratory character' of his experience, Berger has shown with remarkable sensitivity, modern man has suffered from a 'deepening condition of homelessness' (Berger et.al, 1979: 77). It is not at all surprising. Here is a world in which an increasing number of individuals is uprooted from their original social milieu. Not solely that. As Berger adds, 'no succeeding milieu succeeds in becoming truly home either' (Ibid: 165). Yes, a world in which everything is in constant motion is a world in which, to borrow Berger's words, 'certaintanties of any kind are hard to come by' (Ibid: 165).

Yes, this homelessness, it would not be wrong to say,

manifests itself rather strikingly in modern cities. True, as we have already stated, cities are fascinating sites of modernity. In cities things happen: technologies flourish, experimentations take place, market economy grows...But then, cities are also terribly lonely places. In everyday life one encounters innumerable strangers. The anonymity/alienation in this mode of living causes some kind of indifference and hardness. Life tends to lose its warmth, intimacy and spontaneity. Indeed, what Georg Simmel wrote about the metropolis and mental life seems immensely relevant even today. For Simmel, the very act of living in a metropolis causes the 'intensification of nervous stimulation' because of the 'rapid crowding of changing images', or the 'unexpectedness of onrushing impressions'. Furthermore, the predominance of the money economy in the metropolis, adds Simmel, has led to a terribly pragmatic orientation to life.

> Money is concerned only with what is common to all: it asks for the exchange value, it reduces all quality and individuality to the question: How much? All intimate emotional relations between persons are founded in their individuality, whereas in rational relations man is reckoned with like a number, like an element which is in itself indifferent. (Quoted in Bolock and Thompson, 1992: 467)

All this, Simmel would argue, is responsible for the growth of the 'blase attitude'. The mind becomes incapable of discriminating diverse objects. They appear to the blasé person in an evenly flat and gray tone, no one object deserves preference over any other. This invariably implies what Simmel regarded as 'reserve'—cold/heartless indifference.

> We frequently do not even know by sight those who have been our neighbours for years. And it is this reserve which in the eyes of the small town people makes us

appear to be cold and heartless. (Ibid: 468–69).

But then, the search for a new 'home'—a land filled with warmth, intimacy and informality—continues. And we do notice that modernity seeks to evolve new communities: housing societies, literary associations, book clubs, drama groups... And modernity also evolves institutional solutions to the new crisis emanating from the breakdown of the family support system, or the loneliness/suffering of old people. We see the growth of 'old age ashrams', or 'boarding schools'. Yet, despite these modern solutions, there remains a deep-rooted feeling of an absence: absence of a real, living, intimate community. At times, this search leads to a mythical construction of 'lost homes'—the ideal village! Many great Indian minds—from Gandhi to Tagore—often thought of this village, and contrasted its beauty and naturalness from the artificial/contractual relationships prevalent in modern cities. And even today during the festivals—*Holi, Eid* or *Diwali*—one notices the search for this home: people working in cities go back to their ancestral villages: their 'real' homes to celebrate the festive moments. Or, as we are seeing in our times, Hindi films try to reconstruct the 'homeland' for the rootless NRIs! The point we are trying to state is that there is suffering and anguish of the soul—the search for something which has been lost (or something which possibly never existed). Possibly it is this anguish that is often exploited by the fundamentalist politics that wants to go back to the 'roots', and seeks to overcome the 'corrupting' influences of modernity!

Technology, it is said, liberates us. It frees us from the hardship of manual labour, brings comforts, and makes life easy, smooth and efficient. But then, if we think deeply we feel that it also oppresses us. It oppresses us in the sense that it causes excessive indulgence, makes us terribly dependent on the ever-changing needs it creates, and hence paralyzes many important human faculties. Take, for instance, the entry of the ever-expanding technological devices in our everyday life. Instead of evolving a creative relationship with these devices, we tend to become terribly dependent on them. Technology, in fact, evolves its own logic to which we are almost compelled to submit. Progress means getting adjusted to the technological rationale rather than allowing it to listen to our inner voices. No wonder, irrespective of the socio-political system in which we live, we accept the relative autonomy of technology, and begin to equate, say, 'communication' with internet, television and mobile phone, 'seeing' with video camera, 'movement' with cars, and 'standard of living' with technological comforts. This dependence (and this dependence is legitimated in the name of Science and Progress) tends to make us incapable of evolving an alternative mode of living—say, the ability to derive joy in writing a long/hand-written/intimate letter to a friend, the urge to see the sun-set, the changing colour of the sky while walking in silence, or as what Schumacher would have regarded as the willingness to do 'the kind of work that man enjoys most: creative, useful work with hands and brains' (Schumacher, 1983:126). Indeed, I understand why Theodore Roszack equated the technological society with the world's fair in its last days, 'indefinably sad and shady despite the veneer of orthodox optimism' and exhibiting a 'vile thickness' (Roszack, 1972: 64).

In other words, life loses its naturalness; it becomes incapable of seeing beyond the paradigm of technology. Indeed, 'a comfortable, smooth, reasonable, democratic unfreedom', as Herbert Marcuse wrote in his prophetic style, 'prevails in advanced, industrial civilization, a token of technical progress' (Marcuse, 1966:1). It is the irony of the modern age that man is advised to rediscover this 'naturalness' by experts, councillors, psychiatrists and modern physicians. That is why, we witness the frequent warning: do manual work, go in for yoga, jogging and regular exercise, don't watch too much of television, otherwise be ready for high blood pressure, heart disease, diabetes and mental stress. Technology has caused so much indulgence that we now need yet another industry: 'medico-spiritual art of living industry' to teach us the lessons of naturalness! See the suffering. Technology is also making it difficult to live in silence. Man needs silence—contemplative moments to listen to his own inner music. But then, the pathos of modernity is that the 'speed, efficiency and technological smartness' seem to kill this silence. How often I have felt terribly sad looking at my young students. With mobile phones they are talking and talking (nobody knows what they are saying). Meanwhile, they miss the poetry all around: a butterfly roaming around, a bird singing, and the perpetual hide and seek of the sun in a clouded sky. Or, how tragic it is when I see my colleagues driving their cars to the department, while missing a pleasant 20-minute walk! Or, isn't it sad to see young children using only internet to 'download' the learning material, while missing the opportunity to see and explore the world with their own eyes? Had William Wordworth been alive today he would have shared his poetry with us to make us awake:

> *The world is too much with us; late and soon,*
> *Getting and spending, we lay waste our powers:*
> *Little we see in Nature that is ours;*
> *We have given our hearts away, a sordid boon!*
> *This sea that bares her bosom to the moon;*
> *The winds that will be howling at all hours,*
> *And are up-gathered now like sleeping flowers;*
> *For this, for everything, we are out of tune;*
> *It moves us not....*
>
> (Quoted in Bloom and Trilling, 1973: 174)

This seems to be the reason why, despite so many gains of technology, sensitive minds have always warned us of the danger implicit in our excessive dependence on it. Modernity makes us see and adore technological power. Amidst its visibility, bigness and concreteness, seldom do we notice what Schumacher realized with such great sensitivity:

> Strange to say, technology, although of course the product of man, tends to develop by its own laws and principles, and these are very different from those of human nature or living nature in general. Nature always, so to speak knows where and when to stop...There is measure in all natural things—in their size, speed, or violence. As a result, the system of nature of which man is a part, tends to be self-balancing, self-adjusting, self-cleansing. Not so with technology... Technology recognizes no self-limiting principle—in terms, for instance, of size, speed, or violence. It therefore does not possess the virtues of being self-balancing, self-adjusting, and self-cleansing. In the subtle system of nature, technology, and in particular the super technology of the modern world, acts like a foreign body...(Schumacher,1983: 122).

Or, as Herbert Marcuse would have argued, technological rationality creates a totalitarian universe in which there is really no alternative left, because life itself is equated with the gratification of the ever-expanding needs that technology creates. In such an environment 'the people recognize themselves in their commodities; they find their soul in their automobile, hi-fi set, split level home, kitchen equipment, and social control is anchored in the new needs which it has produced' (Marcuse, 1966: 91). Yes, these experiences of suffering, some might argue, touch only the intellectual elite, or the poetic tribe; otherwise, people in general seem to be quite happy with modernity—its technological comforts, the opportunities it provides, and its dynamism, speed and efficiency. Furthermore, it is possible to argue that in a country like ours that has yet to receive all the gains of modernity, speaking of its discontents does not make much sense. That is precisely the problem. If modernity becomes too arrogant to listen to its shortcomings, how can it grow, evolve and become truly self-reflexive?

IV
Complex Trajectory of Indian Modernity

When we look at India we see divergent and complex responses to modernity. It is obvious. Modernity seeks to universalize itself, and no society can remain insulated from it: its core ideals and achievements, and its pain and agony. No wonder, there are adherents as well as critics of modernity. Before we reflect on this spectrum of responses, one thing becomes clear to all of us. Ours is a society that has definitely sought to accomplish the modernist agenda. As historians would argue, the intellectual roots of this agenda could be seen in the making of new India itself: the way we encountered colonialism, coped with the West, critiqued some of the oppressive/traditional practices, engaged in the struggle for de-colonization, marginalized revivalist trends, and evolved a broadly secular/progressive agenda of the freedom struggle which, despite internal differences, celebrated equality, freedom, justice and human dignity (Chandra, 1988). The legacy of this historic struggle that caused grand nationalist consciousness could also be seen in the *Constitution* that the new nation chose as its guiding principle. Indeed, the Constitution as the embodiment of our collective aspirations reveals our willingness to embrace the spirit of modernity: say, the republican spirit in political democracy, acknowledgment of the individual and his/her fundamental rights, an independent judiciary to check the abuse of power, directive principles for social welfare and justice, and moreover, a secular ethos that seeks to resist the tyranny of majoritarianism. This modernity was further intensified by divergent 'nation-making' endeavours. The result was the consolidation of huge modern structures in India: the speedy growth of the techno-industrial infrastructure which Nehru was fond of regarding as 'temples' of new India, proliferation of scientific/professional institutions and universities, massive network of transportation and communication, expansive army structure, and above all, emergence of a new social class trained in modern knowledge systems, and having a 'progressive' orientation to the world. Indeed, the emergent bourgeoisie, the professional middle class and the powerful state celebrating science as the language of development further legitimated modernity as a cherished ideal.

Yes, there was grand expectation from modernity. It was seen as a promise, an emancipatory quest for a new world free from traditional/hierarchical structures and stagnant/ritualistic modes of life. Modernity meant reason, science and development—something that we must incorporate in order to embrace the new age. Not surprisingly, Nehru—the architect of new India—pleaded strongly for a modernist project. He seemed to be a strong believer in modernity—its rationality, its scientific spirit, and its developmental ethos. He saw the devastating consequences of 'the heavy burden of the past'. The condition of 'mental stupor and physical weariness', he didn't hesitate to argue, caused India's degeneration (Nehru, 1983: 54). No wonder, he welcomed the new age, the ethos of reason and scientific method, or, as he put it, 'the adventurous and yet critical temper of science, the search for truth and new knowledge, the refusal to accept anything without testing and trial, the capacity to change previous conclusions in the face of new evidence' (Ibid: 512). Science, for Nehru, ought to be seen as the 'temper of a free man' that we must cultivate in the new age. It was, therefore, quite natural that Nehru could not always agree with the man he otherwise adored most. Yes, Gandhi's moral/spiritual approach, and his critique of some of the principles and practices of modernity, Nehru wrote in his autobiography, did not appeal to him (Nehru, 1984: 504-14). Nehru saw our future in modernity. It may have many problems, but then, it has the capacity to rid itself of those evils. 'We cannot stop the river of change or cut ourselves adrift from it, and psychologically we who have eaten of the apple of Eden cannot forget that taste and go back to primitiveness'. (Ibid: 511).

Yet, Nehru was immensely romantic. He was willing to 'discover' India: not always as a 'modern critic', but as someone eager to understand the mystery of a five thousand year-old civilization. This negotiation with Indian culture and its enduring civilizational structures somewhat softened his modernity. It made him humble. He could appreciate the philosophic depth of the *Upanishads*, the eternal significance of the *Bhagvadgita*, the wisdom of Buddha, or Gandhi's engagement with the masses. The quest for modernity, he realized, should not make us blind to the depth of our civilization.

> Behind and within her battered body one could still glimpse a majesty of soul...Despite the woeful accumulations of superstition and degrading custom that had clung to her and borne her down, she had never wholly forgotten the inspiration that some of the wisest of her children, at the dawn of history, had given her in the *Upanishads*. Their keen minds, ever restless and ever striving and exploring, had not sought refuge in blind dogma or grown complacent in the routine observance of dead forms of ritual and creed. They had demanded not a personal relief from suffering in the present or a place in a paradise to come, but light and understanding: "Lead me from the unreal to the real, lead me from darkness to light, lead me from death to immortality" (Ibid: 429–30).

At this juncture, I wish to make yet another significant point. Nehru's romanticism—or his enthusiasm over the philosophic significance of our great/classical tradition—was not necessarily shared by the victims of history: the marginalized castes and communities. They experienced the hierarchy of caste structure, its trauma and oppression. Any softness, or nostalgic attitude towards our civilization, they might have feared, would reproduce the hegemony of upper caste Hindu ideology. Possibly this led them to strive for modernity, and modernity alone. Its rational/universal ethos, its egalitarianism, and its doctrine of human rights, it was believed, would pose a meaningful challenge to the age-old religious ideology. Look at, for instance, B.R. Ambedkar's uncompromising modernity, his deep-rooted faith in the Enlightenment doctrine of equality, liberty and fraternity, and hence his vehement critique of the philosophy of Hinduism (Ambedkar, 1987). Hinduism, as he argued, upholds privilege and inequality: it means that each man has his vocation preordained; it has, therefore, no relation to capacity nor to innovation. Hinduism, far from spreading knowledge, is a 'gospel of darkness', it refuses the large section of the population of the light of education; moreover, its textual/scriptural form of learning is old-fashioned; it cannot cope with the new age. In other words, Ambedkar posed a rational/modernist critique of the philosophy of Hinduism. Never did Ambedkar feel comfortable with Gandhi. Gandhi, for him, was old-fashioned, a proponent of the *varna* system, and an enemy of modernity. In machinery and technology Ambedkar saw a new hope for the common man. Gandhi's philosophic critique of modernity made no sense to him.

> Gandhism may well be suited to a society which does not accept democracy as its ideal. A society which does not believe in democracy may be indifferent to machinery, and the civilization based upon it. But a democratic society cannot. The former may well content itself with a life of leisure and culture for the few and a life of toil and drudgery for the many. But a democratic

> society must assure a life of leisure and culture to each one of its citizens. If the above analysis is correct then the slogan of a democratic society must be machinery, and more machinery, civilization and more civilization. Under Gandhism the common man must keep on toiling ceaselessly for a pittance and remain a brute. In short, Gandhism with its call of back to nature, means back to nakedness, back to squalor, back to poverty and back to ignorance for the vast mass of the people (Ambedkar, 1998:148).

In other words, modernity, for Ambedkar and his disciples, must play a historic role in India. It must fight casteism and hierarchy, abolish Hinduism, introduce machinery, technology and science for liberating the toiling masses, and create a just society.

Yes, modernity in India, as I have already indicated, is a fact to reckon with. But then, what kind of a modernity is it? Does it fulfill all its promises? Is it like what is broadly known as 'Western modernity' with its technical efficiency, universality and orderly institutional structures? Or, is it chaotic, inefficient, something lagging far behind the developed Euro-American world? True, modernity in India has its own problems and contradictions. We often experience the absence of technical efficiency that a modern society is otherwise proud of. Our banks, hospitals, public institutions and transportation system demonstrate this failure time and again. Institutions collapse; the chaos is all around: when one stands in a long queue in a bank to withdraw money, and discovers with utter dismay that the computer is not working, when doctors fail to entertain patients in a dirty, over-crowded hospital; and when we demonstrate our irresponsibility to public space by reducing it into a sort of garbage. If 'order', 'rational planning' and 'meticulous calculation' characterize the efficiency of modernity, we fail time and again. This failure, every 'modern' Indian feels, is a matter of shame, and a cause of embarrassment, particularly before the foreigners. 'What would they think of us: our chaotic urban centres, our dirty railway stations, our bad roads?—we often ask with a sense of shame and anxiety. Furthermore, we also notice the absence of what is known as professionalism. A universal scale of achievement based on professional aptitude and merit, it is believed, is often scarified, and particularistic criteria based on family/kinship ties acquire undue importance in the selection of teachers, doctors and engineers. Possibly this explains the anguish of a sociologist/historian like Satish Saberwal when he laments that we Indians, because of our confinement to a 'small-scale segmented universe', have proved to be incapable of coping with the requirements of a modern 'mega-society' (Saberwal, 1996). Likewise, it is alleged that because of the heavy weight of traditionalism modernity fails to assert itself. If newness and innovation characterize modernity, we are lagging behind. Because India continues to look 'old' and 'traditional'. Even when the 'youthfulness' of new India is seen in select sites in New Delhi, Bangalore and Chandigarh, you cannot escape the 'old' India—in the streets of Haridwar and Varanasi, in innumerable traditional rituals and customs, in dowry death, female infanticide and caste violence. India has not yet been able to overcome its past. This inertia, it is argued, has done severe damage to our modernity.

In other words, modernity in India has not yet succeeded in presenting itself as 'praise worthy', something that can be compared with 'Western modernity'. This has possibly led a sociologist like Dipankar Gupta to lament, and regard our modernity as 'mistaken modernity' (Gupta, 2000). Modernity, for Gupta, is not just about technology and contemporary artefacts. Modernity, he asserts, means 'dignity of the individual, adherence to universalistic norms, elevation of individual achievement over privileges or dis-privileges of birth, and accountability in public life' (Ibid:

2). As far as these deeper meanings of modernity are concerned, we seem to have failed. Well, there is a move from tradition; but, as Gupta reminds us, we are not yet modern. 'If the clock were to stop here, the final diagnosis would, or rather should, declare India as still un-modern'. (Ibid: 3) He sees no hope in the Indian middle class. It may try to project itself as modern or Western, but it is not truly modern or Western. It is just 'Westoxicated'. 'Unlike westernization, which implies the establishment of universalistic norms and the privileges of achievement over birth, westoxication is about superficial consumerist display of commodities and fads produced in the West' (Ibid: 11). Even though he is not romanticizing the existing Western society, he does not hesitate to conclude that 'in balance, these societies are preferable because they do not discriminate against individuals the way pre-modern societies did and still do'. (Ibid: 16). Gupta wants India to overcome this 'mistaken modernity'. He entertains no ambiguity, and argues that 'there is no alternative but to resolutely press on with the modernist agenda' (Ibid: 13–14).

There is, however, another way of seeing our destiny. It does not necessarily condemn our modernity as 'mistaken'. Instead, it sees the possibility of differences, and reminds us of the specificity of our own modernity. For example, modernity in India need not necessarily be seen as an antithesis of tradition. As a matter of fact, traditional symbols, values and structures have been modernized; and modernity itself has reinforced traditions. For instance, caste, far from withering away, has acquired a new political meaning because of modern democracy. Or, to take yet another illuminating example, Gandhi's life demonstrated how the traditional ideal of a renouncer could be experienced in a modern mass movement. Likewise, modern modes of transportation and communication have intensified religious festivals and pilgrimage. In other words, we see the continual interplay of tradition and modernity (Rudolph and Rudolph, 1967). This distinctiveness of our modernity, it is argued, needs to be appreciated. We need not feel apologetic if our society does not resemble what the West regards as modernity. In fact, as Yogendra Singh has argued, the 'historicity of modernization' is a fact to reckon with (Singh, 1996: 213–15). It should not be forgotten that between tradition and modernity 'a selective process of assimilation and syncretism' occurs. For example, a person who is well-trained in the modern role structure with high instrumental value—say, a surgeon or an engineer or a scientist, may be deeply committed to traditional categorical values. Because, as Singh says, 'categorical values enjoy autonomy over the instrumental values' (Ibid: 214). There is, therefore, no escape from 'the diversity in the pattern of modernization in different societies'.

Yes, modernity in India has its specificity and uniqueness. But then, we should also be careful enough: we need not feel excessively proud of it. In fact, our modernity has also immense problems. How often we have seen that the mobilization of caste for a supposedly radical purpose like 'empowerment' has caused tension-ridden, violent and exclusivist identity politics. We also have seen how at times the doctrine of nationalism and the tyranny of majoritarianism have become almost inseparable. And even though our modernity, as the matrimonial columns suggest, has not destroyed the practice of arranged marriages, we are also witnessing the resurgence of dowry, and an unholy alliance of patriarchy and consumerism. True, we need not find solutions in what is being loosely regarded as a standardized/universal Western modernity. But we have to acknowledge the problems with our own modernity, and think of more innovative and sensitive solutions.

But before we explore these possibilities, it is important to understand that there is also a critical voice amongst us that dislikes the idea of modernity itself, and critiques it relentlessly. They are not old-fashioned traditionalists who regard modernity as an immoral/materialistic/hedonistic life-practice. As a matter of fact, these critics include sophisticated social scientists and refined thinkers. They see the principle of colonial aggression in modernity: the way it annihilates alternative traditions through the ideology of nationalism, scientific planning and mythology of progress. (Nandy, 1987; Madan, 1983). They see the essential dualism in modernity, and resultant violence (Uberoi, 2002). Modernity is being alleged as elitist and anti people. This sort of 'post-colonial' critique of modernity is also being supported by those who speak of subaltern movements: the movements that seek to recover local traditions, indigenous knowledges and subdued/forgotten memories and histories. While modernity is centralizing, these critics plead for fragments and differences (Chatterjee, 1994). Not surprisingly, nationalism, state, science, development—all grand ideals of modernity are suspected. Indeed, we see the assertion of an intellectual milieu characterized by post-colonialism, postmodernism and some sort of reinterpreted Gandhism (Pathak, 1998).

It is not difficult to understand this critique. Because modernity, as we have analyzed, is a complex phenomenon. It has its achievements, promises and possibilities. And it has also its own history of pain, agony and suffering. Modernity is bound to have its adherents as well as its critics. We have to live with this complexity. We have to learn perpetually from this tension and ambiguity, and create a more humane world. One thing is, however, clear. There is no way we can negate modernity completely; the logic of history would not allow it to happen. Furthermore, we are at a stage of evolution when it is no longer possible to live without some of the gains of modernity—its core values, its democratic ethos, or some of its technological achievements. Yet, self-reflexivity demands that we keep our eyes open, explore better possibilities, and retain the courage to innovate. We need not become prisoners of modernity. It is in this context that, I believe, we can learn a couple of lessons from what is being loosely regarded as 'Indian thinking' emanating from visionaries like Sri Aurobindo and Gandhi. This does not mean that we succeed in arriving at immediate and instant alternatives. Possibly we continue to live with our ambiguities. Yet, we must keep this reflexivity alive. Only then is it possible to innovate, and make our contribution to the making of a more humble, dialogic and life-affirming modernity.

First, I wish to recall the lesson we can learn from Sri Aurobindo's profound analysis of the 'curve of the rational age' (Aurobindo, 1977:180–207). Yes, it was the 'revolt of reason' in a modern society that caused one of its remarkable achievements: the creation of individualistic democratic ideal. It was believed that the autonomous individual could question, interrogate, and choose his/her own destiny. But then, reason alone could not create an ideal order. We saw the conflict between the powerful and the powerless; in real terms, individualistic democracy meant, as Sri Aurobindo felt, 'the role of a dominant class over the ignorant, numerous and less fortunate mass' (Ibid: 185). Possibly this discontent led to yet another manifestation of reason: the ideal of democratic socialism. It was, however, no less problematic. It too degenerated into a 'collectivist mystique'. We saw 'a rapid crystallization of the social, economic, political life of the people into a rigid organization' leading to 'a complete unanimity of mind, speech, feel, life'. (Ibid: 193). The message, for Sri Aurobindo, was clear enough. Even though the age of reason was an advance upon the comparative immobility of 'infrarational' societies, it could not arrive at perfection by its own methods, because 'reason is neither the first principle of life, nor can be its last, supreme and sufficient principle' (Ibid: 202). It is high time we realized that no machinery invented by reason could perfect either the individual or the collective man. Neither the market nor the state—the twin symbols of the modern/rational age—can replace what is urgently needed: man's inner transformation. Each of us ought to realize the real source/inspiration behind an ideal/harmonious society: 'the spiritual comradeship of oneness'. Only then is it possible to transcend the conflict between the individual and the collective, and realize the shared divinity that arouses love, brotherhood and solidarity.

> The solution lies not in the reason but in the soul of man, in its spiritual tendencies. It is a spiritual, an inner freedom that alone creates a perfect human order. It is a spiritual, a greater than the rational enlightenment that can illuminate the vital nature of man and impose harmony on its self-seekings, antagonisms and discords (Ibid: 206).

It is indeed true that the central thrust of modernity is towards the mastery of the outer world. It knows how to tap natural resources, create technologies, and evolve mechanical structures to fit the world into its cognitive map. It overemphasizes the role of its scientific/bureaucratic machinery, its market and technology. This excessive inclination to the outer world is like over-emphasizing the vital/physical aspect of the human being. It is filled with terrible *rajasic* energy. But in the process it seems to have forgotten the higher ideal of calmness, inner transformation, and spiritual evolution. That is the crisis of modernity. And, for Sri Aurobindo, it is high time we realized the need of 'the inward view of the East which bids man seek the secret of his destiny and salvation within' (Ibid: 250–51). This spiritual evolution, or this new journey beyond the age of reason does by no means negate the achievements of Western modernity. Because, as Sri Aurobindo repeatedly emphasized, for the pioneers of the new age, nothing would be alien to them, nothing would be outside their scope.

> For every part of human life has to be taken up by the spiritual—not only the intellectual, the aesthetic, the ethical, but the dynamic, the vital, the physical; therefore for none of these things or activities that spring from them will they have contempt or aversion, however they may insist on a change of the spirit and a transmutation of the form (Ibid: 251).

Essentially, this meant a new way of seeing, living and experiencing—a radical shift from the age of reason to the spiritual age. Indeed amidst the noise of the triumphant modernity, it is important to retain a zone of silence, undertake a journey to the inner world, see beyond the stumbling intellectual reason, and experience the light of what the saint regarded as the 'luminous intuitive super-mind'.

Perhaps this discussion would remain incomplete unless you and I recall Gandhi. Yes, it is quite easy to come to an instant conclusion that Gandhi, despite the historic role he played in our freedom struggle, was old-fashioned: someone who could not fit well into the ethos of the new age. Indeed, his insistence on ascetic principles, his inclination to the centrality of the village in our socio-economic life, and his discomfort with modern machine, railways and the legal system might give the impression that Gandhi is irrelevant. As I have already indicated, even Nehru—the disciple and admirer of Gandhi—could not resist expressing his disagreement. He did not seem to feel comfortable with Gandhi's blueprint, his 'glorification of poverty and suffering'. But then, my point of departure is different. What I wish to argue is that it is important to learn from his spirit, not to get obsessed with external forms and symbols. It is desirable to learn from this spirit, use it creatively and alter the trajectory of the prevalent form of modernity. It is in this context that I would make two points.

First, Gandhi's notion of *swaraj* is immensely illuminating. He wanted us to regain the power of 'soul-force', and become independent of the huge techno-economic enterprise of modernity. We have seen how modernity elevates the power of the techno-scientific structure and the nation-state. It is not our contention to deny that these modern structures have made our life easier. But then, these very structures, as we have indicated, have also led to an 'iron cage' or an 'administered totality' that tends to paralyze our own agency and reflexivity. In other words, we become increasingly dependent on the 'expertized' solutions emanating from the techno-bureaucratic elite. This, as Gandhi worried, has belittled man. If I have a problem with my neighbour, I am now incapable of negotiating and arriving at a solution. Instead, I become more and more dependent on an anonymous/impersonal legal structure: its lawyers and courts.

> If people were to settle their own quarrels, a third party would not be able to exercise any authority over them. Truly, men were less unmanly when they settled their disputes either by fighting or by asking their relatives to decide for them. They became more unmanly and cowardly when they resorted to the courts of law. It was certainly a sign of savagery when they settled their disputes by fighting. Is it any the less so, if I ask a third party to decide between you and me? Surely, the decision of a third party is not always right. The parties alone know who is right. We, in our simplicity and ignorance, imagine that a stranger, by taking our money, gives us justice (Gandhi, 1989: 51).

Likewise, if I fall sick, I am incapable of looking after myself, and altering my life-project. Instead, I begin to rely more and more on the medical expert. Indeed, 'the doctors induce us to indulge, and the result is that we have become deprived of self-control, and have become effeminate. (Ibid:

53–54). Gandhi sought to alter it. He thought that we must cultivate our 'soul force'—our moral/spiritual power—to revitalize ourselves, our villages, and our communities. In a way, Gandhi's notion of swaraj was far deeper, not just the replacement of one kind of authority by the other.

Second, Gandhi felt that the modern civilization was based on the centrality of *desire*. It cultivates and stimulates man's desire for the ever-expanding needs, and never-ending comforts. Yes, we do indeed become prisoners of these comforts. This causes perpetual restlessness for more and more.

> We notice that the mind is a restless bird; the more it gets the more it wants, and still remains unsatisfied. The more we indulge our passions the more unbridled they become. Our ancestors, therefore, set a limit to our indulgences. They saw that happiness was largely a mental condition. A man is not necessarily happy because he is rich, or unhappy because he is poor...Observing all this, our ancestors discarded us from luxuries and pleasures...(Ibid: 55).

Even though it is naive to imagine that we can go back to the world in which our ancestors lived, the essence of what he was saying needs to be understood. This excessive desire, we should not forget, has two disastrous consequences: *(a)* it deprives one of evolving a zone of peace, and *(b)* it violates the ecological principle: a harmonic engagement between man and nature. Gandhi critiqued this 'immoral' or 'satanic' force which contemporary critics often regard as the seduction of consumer culture. He was thinking of a life: truly independent in the sense that it is not a slave of desire. This is possibly the other meaning of *ahimsa*. Yes, modernity has indeed done a lot of good things; but it has also caused severe damage to our life and environment. We moderns would lose nothing except our arrogance if we learn a couple of lessons from Gandhi's visionary insight.

V
Realm of Possibilities

Am I expecting the impossible? It may be alleged that while I wish to get all good things of modernity, I seek to avoid its negative consequences. It may be argued that if I adopt the spirit of freedom, individuation and critical consciousness, I must be willing to pay a price—an experience of homelessness, or alienation from the community. Or, if I wish to be benefitted by science and technology, I must be ready to accept the inevitability of power—the power emanating from the specialized discourse of scientists and technocrats. Yes, I am aware of the complexity of living; nothing is possible to achieve without bearing some of its unintended consequences. Yet, I would argue that with sufficient self-reflexivity it is possible to have a more creative mode of living and a network of social institutions.

It is in this context that I wish to speak of the possibility of transcending the duality of freedom and relatedness, rebellion and love, and individual and community. As I have already stated, a major achievement of modernity is that it inspires us to privilege the spirit of freedom: the criticality to question and interrogate. But then, this quest need not necessarily be seen as an expression of duality: my science vs. their religion, my rationality vs. their communitarianism, my progressiveness vs. their conservatism. I critique and resist, but my criticality is not necessarily hostility; it can be an urge to involve even those I am revolting against, and to try—as collective subjects—to alter the world. In other words, criticality can also be experienced as a dialogic engagement; freedom can be seen as a higher form of relatedness, and individuality as an articulation of an enriched community. Kabir, for instance, critiqued orthodoxy; he did not become an alien outsider; he became everybody's Kabir. Gandhi's 'experiments' did not prevent him from remaining a Hindu. And even young Marx saw communism as a transcendence of all dualities.

> It is the genuine resolution of the conflict between man and nature and between man and man—the true resolution of the strife between existence and essence, between objectification and self-confirmation, between freedom and necessity, between the individual and the species (Marx, 1977: 97).

This is what I regard as an urge to *spiritualize* modernity. We should not negate it as merely utopian. Instead, we must try to live, and experience it. I believe that a new sensitivity is evolving, and it is nice to see Roy Bhaskar—the proponent of *critical realism*—striving for the same experience:

> Now if you take the ideal from Mahayana Buddhism of the Bodhisattva, he may be the most realized human being but he will postpone his enlightenment, his own bliss, his own *nirvana* until the realization of every other being in the world. That is very similar to the standpoint of Marx—and Marx was an atheist—when he said that in a communist society the free development of each would be the condition of the free development of all. In other words, your well-being, your flourishing was the condition for mine...That is also precisely the standpoint of Buddhism. And if you go into it deeply enough, at some level, this is the standpoint of all great religions and also even political inspirations and aspirations... There is no contradiction between spirituality and radical social change (Bhaskar, 2002:301).

Likewise, it is important to see beyond scientism and relativism. And I would argue that it is possible. Yes, I have already spoken of the danger of scientism. I am also aware that contemporary postmodernism delegitimizes science, and celebrates multiplicity of narratives without privileging any of these as the master truth. Possibly there is an element of relativism in the postmodern doctrine of heterogeneity. But then, the point I am trying to put forward is that it is possible as well as desirable to affirm science in its appropriate context without being indifferent to other possibilities in different domains. Let me give an example. Once I met with an accident, and my right elbow was displaced and severely fractured. I chose to consult a modern orthopaedic surgeon. I legitimated his scientific knowledge of complex surgery, because I did not believe that the other traditions like *unani* or *ayurveda* could have helped me. But then, I am aware that there are contexts in which alternative medicines work, and work brilliantly. So while I can safely go to an orthopaedic surgeon for a complex elbow surgery, I can listen to immensely devotional *bhajan* songs to relax my mental stress, and take *tulsi* and *neem* to save myself from common cold and fever. In other words, it is possible to live while creating multiple sites for diverse traditions. Modernity then becomes humble, open and inclusive—not something characterized by the certainty/dogma/hegemony of modern science.

All this implies that I am speaking of the ability to distinguish *enabling* technology from a ruthlessly technologized culture. I would give an example from my own experiential domain. I have not yet bought a car. I do not undermine the significance of cars. I, however, insist that the idea that every middle class professional must have his own car reflects a culture in which technology tries to salvage the atomized individual. Possibly we need more and more improved modes of public transportation and roads that, far from being just car-friendly, are accommodative, and allow a dignified space for those who love to walk, or who are fond of bicycles. I would imagine a radical form of urban designing that would not compel one to buy a car. What I wish to suggest is that technologies can be used meaningfully and creatively, and not in a way that non-technical solutions become redundant. It is really sad to see that technological indulgence has acquired such intensity that we now need yet another form of bureaucratic/legal control—say, the ban on the use of mobile phones at schools. Why should we allow ourselves to reach such a stage? Mobile phones can be used by a doctor, by a police official, or sometimes even by ordinary people like us for absolutely emergency needs. But when a school kid cannot imagine his existence without it, when television channels receive nothing but SMS messages from the viewers, and when in application forms one is asked to give one's mobile number, one realizes that technology, far from liberating us, has killed our imagination. Life is essentially a delicate art, not a technological spectacle. And our modernity must learn it.

Let me give yet another example relating to our engagement with nature. Nature is extraordinarily complex—full of ambiguities. Nature is abundantly beautiful. Nature nurtures and sustains us. Nature arouses poetry and adoration—a sense of humility, and an urge to pray. I often recall the *Vedic* hymns, and experience the beauty of this enchantment.

> *Upward, O Agni, rise thy flames, pure and resplendent, blazing high.*
> *Thy lustres, fair effulgences.* (RV.VIII: 44.17)
>
> *Bless us with shine, bless us with perfect day light, bless us with cold, with fervent heat and lustre.*
>
> *Bestow on us, O Surya, varied riches, to bestow us in our home and when we travel* (RV. X: 37.10)

I am, however, aware that nature is not just beautiful; it is no less violent, unpredictable and destructive. Possibly the very logic of survival has led man to discover the science of *conquering* nature. It is seen rather strikingly in the Beconian understanding of nature, in the Cartesian duality of body and mind, and in ruthless technological development. But then, as history suggests, this techno-scientific enterprise often becomes a monster. It loses control over itself. It seeks to conquer everything. Big dams displace people, industries pollute the environment, and malls colonize the urban space. I am not suggesting that science is unimportant, and we should surrender before nature. But it is definitely possible to have a sense of humility, and relate to nature in a more complex and creative fashion. It is like recognizing 'core ecological values' like *(a)* live in harmony with nature, *(b)* overcome anthropocentric prejudice, and *(c)* recognize intrinsic value in beings other than humans (Hayward, 1994).

And finally, I wish to speak of participatory institutions. I have already indicated that it is important to acknowledge the crisis emanating from the dynamics of power in modern institutions. Take, for instance, the overwhelming power of schools in modern societies. Schools seek to monopolize the domain of knowledge, and one is almost led to believe that without schools there is no learning. Schools process knowledge and people, schools measure one's morality, emotion and cognition; and schools—with their characteristic rituals of examination and time-table—have almost absolute control over the child's body and mind. Likewise, modern medicine is yet another discourse of power. Big hospitals with their characteristic anonymity, doctors with their super-specialization, and sophisticated medical gadgets which perpetually fragment and objectify the human body have made it almost impossible for a patient to have a meaningful engagement with the medical establishment. From the birth of a baby to one's death at the ICU in a mega hospital—everything is now monitored and recorded.

I am not suggesting that these discourses of power are only negative and repressive. There is indeed a positive and productive dimension of power. After all, we know something at schools, and doctors do cure us. But then, it is possible to restructure these institutions. One way of doing it is to introduce a great deal of freedom and choice. And then, as Leo Tolstoy imagined, 'the school will, perhaps, not be a school as we understand it,—with benches, blackboards, a teacher's or professor's platform,—it may be a panorama, a theatre, a library, a museum, a conversation' (Tolstoy, 1967:15). Likewise, doctors would begin to combine the technicality of medicine and the art of human conversation to evolve a more integral practice of healing, and patients would overcome their stigmatized identities and acquire a meaningful voice in deciding the way they wish to live and die. This is to strive for more participatory, humane and dialogic institutions.

This journey to a decentralized, ecological, humane, reflexive and humble modernity need not be seen as utopian. Yes, it is an exceedingly challenging task. But it is not impossible, provided we want it with absolute zeal and sincerity. What else is modern, if not the enthusiasm to experiment and innovate?

2

Art of Resistance in the Era of Cultural Globalization

How we respond to modernity is indeed a challenge. But then, time is changing fast, and we are confronting yet another challenge: how to cope with globalization—a process that seeks to overcome all borders and boundaries, and brings the world closer economically and culturally, a process in which, as Giddens would argue, social relations are constructed 'across infinite spans of time-space' (Giddens, 1990: 21). It is true that globalization is a logical consequence of modernity itself. Because modernity, as it originated in the West, is inherently universalizing in nature. Its science knows no borders; its technology transcends territorial boundaries; and its politico-cultural aspirations—democratization of society, and the autonomy of the individual—tend to become our shared aspirations. But then, what we call globalization, despite its roots in modernity, acquires a new meaning and momentum in our times. Globalization, therefore, needs special attention. It is in this context that I wish to mention two specific characteristics of globalization.

First, the age of modernity, it should not be forgotten, was also an age of the nation-state, its assertion and sovereignty, its primary role in the making of the destiny of people situated in a political collective called the 'nation'. It was also an epoch in which de-colonization movements all over the world gave confidence to the newly independent nations to retain their autonomy. It was a period of socialism, non-alignment and alternative cultures that could resist the hegemony of global capitalism. Yes, because of the universalizing nature of modernity, particularly the expansionist capitalist market, there was also an aspiration for the standardized international culture. But then, as Hobsbawm wrote, it remained limited only to the 'numerically modest middle class and some of the rich' because 'the world capitalist system was a structure of rival national economies' (Hobsbawm, 2004). Things are, however, changing in recent times. The socialist alternative seems to have collapsed; the memory of de-colonization, many would argue, is fading away; non-alignment is often said to be irrelevant in the post-Cold War era, and transnational economic corporations are altering the traditional notion of the sovereignty of the nation. As Sklair argues, we are witnessing 'the establishment of a borderless global economy, the complete denationalization of all corporate procedures and activities, and the eradication of economic nationalism (Sklair, 2004). This is not to suggest that the nation-state has become altogether irrelevant. As a matter of fact, the nation-state continues to play an important role in issues relating to law and order, international negotiation and defence. What, however, cannot be denied is that as the world is fast integrating itself with the logic of the global capitalist market, the nation-state is losing its hold. It seems to be an unconditional surrender before the IMF/World Bank mantra of globalization which, as innumerable studies suggest, has by no means helped developing countries to have the ability, freedom and flexibility, to make strategic choices in finance, trade and investment policies' (Kher, 2001; Stiglitz, 2003).

Second, a dramatic change has taken place in the domain of information technology. With audio-visual transmissions, digital television, computer networks, satellites, faxes and portable phones, global communication—the dissemination of information, messages and symbols across the world—has become much easier, and the nation-state can no longer be said to be the sole master in shaping one's cultural trajectory. Not solely that. Information technologies greatly facilitate capital mobility and speed of transaction, and make the historic transformation possible: from a mere 'world economy' to a truly 'global economy'. As Castells writes:

> The information economy is global. A global economy is historically new reality, distinct from a world economy. A world economy, that is an economy in which capital accumulation proceeds throughout the world, has existed in the West at least since the sixteenth century, as Fernand Braudel and Immanuel Wallerstein have taught us. A global economy is something different: it is an economy with the capacity to work as a unit in real time on a planetary scale. While the capitalist mode of production is characterized by its relentless expansion, always trying to overcome limits of time and space, it is only in the late twentieth century that the world economy was able to become truly global on the basis of the new infrastructure provided by information and communication technologies. This globality concerns the core processes and elements of the economic system (Quoted in Mc Guigan, 1999: 108).

In this context it is also important to realize that in our times social and geographical mobility has increased immensely. In fact, as Urry reminds us:

> At the beginning of the twenty first century there are well over 700 million movements, across international borders each year (compared with twenty five million in 1950); at any time 300,000 passengers are in flight above the USA, equivalent to a substantial city; there are thirty one million refugees and 100 million international migrants worldwide; and international

> travel, which constitutes the largest movement of people across borders that has ever occurred, accounts for over one twelfth of world trade (Urry, 2003:.61).

Indeed, with widespread tourism, migration and rising diasporic communities, cultures are continually overlapping, and together with economic globalization, a fluid/hybrid global culture has begun to emerge. Globalization, therefore, needs special attention. True, globalization cannot be imagined without modernity. But then, globalization gives a new meaning to modernity. It is the modernity of the post-Cold War/post-socialist era characterized by the overwhelming power of the market, information revolution and heightened social mobility. And India, it goes without saying, is no exception. It cannot escape the ongoing global process. As we are witnessing in the neo-liberal phase of economic globalization, the self-perception of the Indian state is undergoing a dramatic transformation. The Nehruvian era that sought to privilege the agency of the nation-state in unfolding people's socio economic welfare, political commentators have begun to argue, is fast becoming a thing of the past. As the critical voice asserts, the politico-economic implications of globalization are not always conducive to the project of an egalitarian India.

> The state in India, instead of occupying centre-stage in social and economic arenas, is seen to be in retreat. This is obvious in the economic sphere from which it has been retreating over more than two decades now and, of course, most dramatically since 1991–92. But it is also true in the social sphere in matters such as providing opportunities to the minorities, the backward classes, tribal communities and women and children, encouraging people's initiatives and indigenous thinking in key areas such as education, environment, health and housing, and generally implementing the

> laws of the land for the betterment of the poorer and oppressed sections of society (Kothari, 1995:1595).

But then, it is not just the question of economic globalization and its political consequences. We are also witnessing the dramatic socio-cultural transformation in India—the steady growth of the middle class with global aspirations, the spread of consumptionist culture, the revolution in mass media and information technology, and the changing mode of entertainment, leisure and lifestyle. Yes, India is a complex society that lives in many worlds simultaneously. While global cultural symbols are distinctively visible in the urban/metropolitan social milieu, people in villages, or in urban fringes, it may be argued, are so preoccupied with everyday struggle for survival that they are seldom touched by these changes. What I, however, wish to add is that even though the influences of globalization are uneven, its significance can by no means be undermined. In fact, global aspirations and symbols are entering everywhere: Pepsi/Coke can be seen at a village teashop, cable TV constitutes an important component of slum culture, and beauty parlours are no less popular in small towns. In other words, globalization is leading to a significant change in the cultural landscape. India must learn to cope with this changing reality. Yes, we have already written about modernity. But then, as I have indicated, modernity itself has acquired a new meaning in the global era. We ought to evolve meaningful ways to cope with these new challenges.

I
Why Culture?

In this chapter, however, I wish to concentrate on cultural globalization. Enough has already been said and written about economic globalization—its promises as well as its discontents. But the phenomenon called cultural globalization is equally an important issue that needs to be understood and reflected upon. Because it is in the domain of culture that we think, express ourselves, articulate our aspirations and anxieties, and decide the mode of life we wish to engage in. In other words, it is our culture—its ideals, symbols and everyday practices, its rites, rituals and festivals—that distinguishes us, and defines our humanity. No wonder, culture remains an intimate zone. We breathe and smell our culture. It gives us our distinctive identity. It is this emotive engagement with our culture that also causes an acute anxiety. We often feel that if we lose our culture, we lose our uniqueness, our specificity, and our own contributions to human civilization.

Yes, there are multiple cultures that have given distinctive identities to multiple communities, and created a world characterized by the diversity of religious rituals, sexual practices, dietary habits and aesthetic modes. Even if, as part of nature, we all eat, drink, sleep and copulate, our ways of fulfilling these biological needs are different, and essentiality culturally loaded. No wonder, it is we, not the other species, who debate on 'right' or 'wrong' food, 'sacred' space or 'profane' objects, 'appropriate' sex or 'inappropriate' desire. In fact, 'the only way we can know the significance of the selected detail of behaviour', wrote Ruth Benedict, 'is against the background of the motives and emotions and values that are institutionalized in that culture' (Benedict, 1971: 35). As a matter of fact, there is no other way to understand—if I am allowed to take some examples at random—why, for the Hindus, a river like the Ganga no longer remains simply a river, but becomes sacred; why, as Margaret Mead showed, the process of growing up of Samoan children is strikingly different from that of American children; or why, as Malinowski would have argued, the Victorian sexual morality did not have much significance among the Trobriand Islanders.

But then, this diversity does by no means suggest that cultures are destined to remain insulated. It is true that cultures have their own specific contexts: ethnic communities, linguistic groups, religious associations, territorial boundaries and even modern nations. It is also true that cultures do have an immense power of resilience. Yet, the idea of a 'pure and eternally stable culture', I wish to argue, is more mythical than real. Cultural boundaries are not like iron walls. Instead, cultures often meet, interact, overlap and overcome ethnic/linguistic/territorial boundaries. For example, if we look at our own history, even in ancient times we could see the spread of culture and religion—say, Ashoka's children going to what is now known as Sri Lanka to spread Buddhism; Hiuen Tsang, the Chinese Buddhist, visiting India in the seventh century A.D, and engaging with the prevailing culture; or Christianity coming to Kerala way back in the fourth century A.D. Likewise, in the medieval period we saw the confluence of Hinduism and Islam in the changing cultural landscape that reflected itself in music, architecture, language and religion. And in modern times we have witnessed a sustained interaction of cultures leading to the dissemination of the discoveries of science, liberal democracy and nationalism all over the world. Because of this ongoing interaction, Urdu and English, Christmas and Id, tea and Mughlai, and cricket and cinema have become integral components of our cultural practice. Cultures are continually expanding their horizon.

Yet, this interaction is not necessarily a simple, non-problematic phenomenon. In fact, when cultures meet and interact, there is also a politics. Because cultures may have asymmetrical resources emanating from the unequal distribution of wealth and political power, and the resultant interaction may be characterized by conquest, domination, subjugation and marginalization. I wish to give a concrete example from the cultural politics of colonialism. Because we did experience the domination and superiority of the colonial masters: the way their masculinity, racial origin, religion and science were projected as superior to the culture of the colonized. The hidden assumption, as I have already mentioned in the earlier chapter, was that the colonial masters—through their school teachers, religious missionaries and efficient administrators—could 'civilize' the 'effeminate' race of the colonized. As a matter of fact, this hierarchy could be seen in the politics of anthropology itself. Because anthropology was born to discover the 'other' of White/Christian/Modern West in 'primitive/non-literate' cultures (say the Orient, the Dark Continent, the South Seas, and the Amazonian jungle). It was essentially a hierarchical vision of the world divided between civilization and primitivity, 'we' and 'they' (Madan, 1996). Yes, it was not just about the narration of cultural differences; it was also about hierarchizing these differences: 'modern' vs 'primitive', 'science' vs. 'magic', and 'reason' vs. 'superstition'. It privileged the Western anthropologist to write about, and essentialize other cultures and traditions. But then, it has to be admitted that cultural anthropology as a discipline is engaging itself in a self-reflexive exercise. And possibly the spirit of de-colonization characterized by the assertion of multiple voices has led anthropology to redefine its agenda. Jonathan Friedman captures this moment when he writes:

> The increasing insecurity of the anthropologist in the fragmenting hegemony of the world system has led to a breakdown of what is new referred to as a former 'ethnographic authority'. Culture is now understood as a text, often a reification of another 'way of life', which ought to be understood as a negotiated result rather than a reflection of an objective or described reality. This is often driven home by the fact that those whom anthropologists study now speak for themselves, represent their own lives and don't easily consent to anthropologists 'speaking' or 'writing' them (Friedman, 1999: 71–72).

But then, this kind of dialogic interaction of cultures was not easy in the colonial context which, because of its very nature, was hierarchical. Well, it is possible to argue that an encounter with the mighty colonial power enabled the colonized to widen their horizon, look at themselves, their mistakes and follies, and to become more self-reflexive. And at the same time, as cultural historians have written (Raychaudhuri, 1987), it caused severe anxiety: the fear of being dominated and marginalized. Interestingly and paradoxically, this experience of humiliation also led to the recovery of one's own culture for self-respect and identity. Gandhi's life-trajectory, to take a historic illustration, revealed this process rather sharply: change and continuity, the willingness to learn from others, yet the courage to retain one's own identity (Parekh, 1989). Gandhi did not always give his consent to the central premises of post-Enlightenment European modernity. In a way, he was deeply rooted in his own culture-in the discourses of the *Bhagvadgita* and the *Upanishads,* and in the rhythm of what he loved to regard as 'self-sufficient' Indian villages. Yet, culture, for him, was not something fixed and closed forever. Instead, his cross-cultural conversation could be seen the way this *sanatani* Hindu learned from Christianity, from Tolstoy, Ruskin and Thoreau, and made innumerable 'experiments' in his own life and culture. It revealed the very complexity of cultural interaction: its politics, its ambiguities, and its possibilities.

The interaction of cultures is, therefore, a complex phenomenon. First, it indicates that cultures, although situated in specific ethno-national contexts, often overcome territorial/national borders and boundaries. Cultures, despite the power of resilience, can prove to be elastic, dynamic, flexible and, therefore, living. Second, the interaction of cultures, as history suggests, is not necessarily always a symmetrical one. Instead, it can be characterized by domination and subjugation: say, the West seeking to dominate the East or the Hindus trying to 'integrate' the tribals into their own fold! Third—and this is the most important point—culture is also a site of protest and a zone of creative experimentation. While it seeks to assert, renew and innovate itself in order to resist domination, and retain its specificity and autonomy, it also evolves a dialogic space, and strives for the fusion of horizons. In other words, cultures need not necessarily be hostile to one another. Cultures may try to merge, and we may progress towards a more shared, open and inclusive culture.

It is in this context that cultural globalization acquires added significance. Because it means more speedy and sustained interaction of cultures—the intensity of which, as I have already indicated, we didn't experience earlier. That is why, new questions and anxieties begin to confront us: Who are we? What is our culture? Does globalization enrich our culture, and make it more fluid and flexible? Can we exist as an equal partner in the globalizing process? Or, do we lose amidst what is being critiqued as 'cultural imperialism'? Can we survive, resist, experiment and innovate? Can we evolve an appropriate *art of resistance* to cope with the changing times, and live with delicacy, symmetry and creativity?

II
Nuances of Cultural Globalization

A question, however, needs to be answered. Once economic globalization is understood, is there any other reason to pay attention to cultural globalization? One is often tempted to equate culture with a mere epiphenomenon: something that is being solely determined by the economy. But then, as I would argue, the relationship between economic and cultural globalization, far from being purely deterministic, is multi-layered. It is more complex, and hence more interesting. There are four dimensions to it.

First, there is indeed a significant influence of the economy over culture. For example, if the economy is globalized, and the rationality of the market becomes overwhelmingly powerful, culture too begins to 'free' itself from territorial/nationalist boundaries. If I live amidst the continual flow of foreign goods and transnational corporations, if I accept that the market need not bother about boundaries because it is 'universal', why should I remain emotionally attached to the 'local' product? Possibly I would not feel so bad to devalue my own *lemon water* and *lassi*, and switch over to the more 'trendy' Pepsi or Coke, or why should I remain confined to my 'national' car: say, the Ambassador from the Hindustan Motors, when corporate banks are willing to give me loans to buy any brand of 'international' car I like? No wonder, global 'brands'—Nike, Apple, Pepsi-Cola, Benetton, Body Shop, Virgin, Swatch, Calvin Klein, Sony and Starbucks roam the globe, and enter our inner world. Furthermore, I need to orient myself to survive in the 'free' global market; I need to evolve a taste and aptitude to promote and sustain the ever-expanding market. No wonder, the economic globalization would require a consumptionist/market-oriented/competitive culture (Sklair, 1991). Let me give an example from my own experiential domain. The Priya Complex in posh Vasant Vihar colony in New Delhi is not far from the university where I teach. It is, as the new generation believes, a 'happening' place that reveals the seduction of the global market. Indeed, as I move around, I notice the glimpses of cultural globalization: young boys and girls wearing Levi's/ Nautica jeans, using their credit cards to withdraw money from the ATM counter, shopping around, consuming McDonald's hamburger, and seeing Hollywood films in the gorgeous theatre hall. I smell the market—its style, intoxication and packaging.

I am not talking merely about the market place. Economic globalization does not spare even the site of education. A welfare state promoting a culture-sensitive education, many would fear, is fast becoming a thing of the past. Instead, economic liberalization/globalization leads to the proliferation of more and more international schools, private institutions and teaching shops selling market-friendly education: management, information technology and fashion designing! A leading proponent of economic globalization in India celebrates this moment with great enthusiasm when he writes:

> Few realize that 54 per cent of Indians today are less than 25 years of age. And they matter: the average age of the ones who are creating Rs.60,000 crores worth of wealth every year in Information Technology is just 26 years! These youngsters care little for the rhetoric of our doomsayers. They are not afraid of the world. They feel they can out-do the competition. They know they have outdone the competition in field after field. They just want the freedom to do so. They just want the wherewithal, the environment—precisely the things that Reforms bring about—to do so (Shourie, 2004).

Indeed, the reflections of cultural globalization are noticed in this new 'confidence', the way the Government of India once regarded it as 'a revolution in which the world says 'hello' to India': the assertion of the new middle class, the proliferation of shopping malls in our cities, the growing popularity of tourism packages for Singapore and Dubai, the changing pattern of consumption, the craze for privatization, and the urge to see everything, be it school or hospital, as a market-friendly industry.

Second, it can be argued that the two domains—economy and culture—can retain their relative autonomy. It is like believing that even if there is reason to celebrate economic globalization, it is possible to retain the autonomy and specificity of our culture. Culture need not lose its historicity and its core values in the name of being globalized. In fact, the urge to retain the autonomy of culture, despite techno-economic changes, is not a recent phenomenon. At a time when we were encountering colonial modernity, it was felt that, despite the arrival of science, technology and industry, we could retain our specific cultural values. In other words, it was felt that culture ought to be seen as a 'sacred' domain, not to be touched by the changes in the economy. Techno-economic progress and cultural heritage, it was hoped, could go together. This 'national-cultural' project, Partha Chatterjee has shown brilliantly, could be seen in, say, Bankim Chandra Chatterjee's celebration of 'a cultural ideal in which the industries and sciences of the West can be learnt and emulated while retaining the spiritual greatness of Eastern culture' (Chatterjee, 1986: 73). As a matter of fact, this 'national-cultural' project can be seen even now when we notice the Hindu Right seeking to reconcile economic globalization with cultural nationalism. Not surprisingly, it is argued that I need not have any problem in inviting transnational corporations in the economy, I can leave my country, and work in a software company in the USA, and I can support the supremacy of the USA in the global politics; yet, I can feel proud of being a Hindu and an Indian! This cultural nationalism amidst economic globalization can be seen in the NRI phenomenon: its affinity with cultural symbols or its search for 'roots'. It can also be seen in the production and dissemination of cultural goods—say, popular films like *Hum Apke Hain Kaun* and *Kal Ho Naa Ho,* and television serials like *Saas Bhi Kabhi Bahu Thi* and *Des Mein Nikla Hoga Chand*—that sancitify the norms of the Hindu extended family, arranged marriages and religious practices amongst those who otherwise live in a global corporate world, and are extremely wealthy and mobile.

In fact, this urge to separate the economy and culture has got yet another interesting consequence. It is like believing that one can resist economic globalization while practising cultural globalization. As Madhu Kishwar wrote in her usual provocative style, there are revolutionaries—leftists, NGO activists, feminists and environmentalists—who are 'globally connected', teach in Euro-American universities, speak English, and retain almost an American standard of living; yet, they are the ones who fight relentlessly against global capitalism, the IMF-WTO nexus and the American imperialism (Kishwar, 2004). Almost in a similar fashion Urry has argued that all these new organizations are globally mediated; people imagine themselves as members/supporters of such organizations 'through purchases, wearing the T-shirts, hearing the CD, surfing the organizations page on the Web, participating in computerized jamming and so on'(Urry, 2003: 90). In other words, here is a situation characterized by a high degree of ambiguity.

Third, it is thought that culture is a domain having immense possibilities. It can create a new language of resistance. It can resist economic as well as cultural globalization, and oppose a trend towards homogenization. It is like tapping cultural resources, indigenous knowledges, arousing the collective sentiment, articulating the danger of imperialism in the 'neo-liberal order', and evolving cultural symbols to fight the hegemony of Americanization. This passion, it seems, has lead Arundhati Roy to recall Gandhi's Salt March—the way it was a 'direct strike at the economic underpinning of the British Empire', and to plead for yet another non-cooperation movement to resist globalization or what she regards as the American hegemony.

> Our resistance has to begin with a refusal to accept the legitimacy of the US occupation of Iraq. It means acting to make it materially impossible for Empire to achieve its aims. It means soldiers should refuse to fight, reservists should refuse to serve, workers should refuse to load ships and aircraft with weapons...I suggest

> that... we choose, by some means, two of the major corporations that are profiting from the destruction of Iraq. We could then list every project they are involved in. We could locate their offices in every city and every country across the world. We could go after them. We could shut them down. It is a question of bringing our collective wisdom and experience of past struggles to bear on a single target. It's a question of the desire to win (Roy, 2004).

In a project of this kind culture is being seen as a site of protest. It is believed that one can redefine cultural symbols, and fight the prevalent practices of economic and cultural globalization.

Fourth, there is also a creative possibility of adaptability, innovation and experimentation. It is argued that there is something irreversible in the globalizing process, and there is also something good about it. It is, therefore, desirable to remain open, and strive for reconciliation. It is possible to have cultural diffusion and hybridity. Not solely that. It is argued that there is no reason to grow panicky, and fear that globalization would invariably destroy local cultures. Instead, local cultures, far from withering away, would renew themselves through global exchange. This would lead to what Robertson once regarded as 'glocalization' (Robertson, 1995). In fact, a leading Indian sociologist wanted us to see this creative possibility:

> The new means of communication also augment and empower the local communities, local cultures and minority sects by extending the reach of their interactions. Their cultural and emotional bonds are strengthened due to their global reach through new telecommunication linkages, e.g., video-meetings, tele-discussions etc... Apart from such empowering impact, the local communities and cultures are also inspired by the new telecommunication media to reassert their

> cultural identity and reinforce their resilience. It helps them maintain their identity by accessing themselves to cultural meanings and values rather selectively through an adaptive mechanism (Singh, 2000: 59–60).

Here one sees the possibility of a creative interplay of the global and the local. Not solely that. Far from denouncing hybridity, one sees its innate aliveness and experimental ethos.

In fact, all these four approaches suggest that culture has indeed become an important site of enquiry. And new questions have begun to emerge. Is globalization the other name of cultural imperialism? Or, is there a liberating potential in what is often being seen as the irreversible process of globalization? Can our culture/cultures innovate and survive without regressing to fundamentalism and conservatism?

III
Expanded Horizon: A New Possibility

As I look at the world and experience it, I negotiate with these diverse approaches to cultural globalization. I know that my own engagement with cultural globalization is immensely complex. It has its own story of approval and rejection. In fact, the art of resistance I wish to propose would emerge out of this complex and critical engagement.

To begin with, I must concede that there is something inherently positive about globalization, if it truly widens my horizon, and makes me familiar with the larger world, its diversity and multiple colours. True, my little world, my culture, my language, my rituals and symbols assure me, and give me a sense of belonging and security. I find myself amidst those who too are like me and thinking like me. But then, this little/stable world can also be a source of confinement, because this insulation does not help me evolve and grow. That is why, when the boundaries become fuzzy and fluid and cultures begin to interact more rapidly, the currents of the larger world are likely to cause temporary disturbance: some kind of insecurity, anxiety and restlessness. Yet, if I can bear it, retain my balance, and learn from this exchange of cultures, I begin to evolve, grow, mature, and broaden my universe. It is like opening up my mind, rediscovering the larger world around me, and acquiring the courage to look at my world even through the eyes of the others, and transform it.

The speedy interaction with the world that globalization stimulates does indeed help. Everything, be it football or cultural heritage, is reinterpreted. Take my own case—my process of growing up in West Bengal in the 1970s. I lived in a 'make-believe' world, and felt that the ultimate meaning of football was nothing but the performance of my favourite team in Kolkata. But with the coming of globalization and its implicit telecommunication revolution, one day I got a remote in my hand and everything began to change. I could now move to any sports channel I liked, and watch 'world football'—the speed, thrill and professionalism of *Manchester United, Arsenel* and *Chelsea.* It made me realize that we ought to do a great deal of work to improve our own football. As a matter of fact, this exposure has become more real and more intense. We now know the world not simply through the texts written by distant scholars, historians and travellers. Now, thanks to globalization, ordinary people like us move around the world, and experience it more frequently and more intensely. So when my nephew visits Europe, and narrates the extraordinary story of preserving and maintaining the museums and art galleries in Paris, Berlin and Amsterdam, I do realize that we need to learn from them: their historic sense and their responsibility to collective heritage. This is indeed a gain of globalization: it makes one realize that not everything is fine in one's own culture. The result is that it leads to dynamism and innovation—the willingness to cope with the world. It is in this sense that globalization breeds the ever-expanding reference groups. As a matter of fact, the entire world becomes a mirror through which we begin to look at ourselves: our modes of living, our art and entertainment, sports and leisure, and science and religion. That is why, we cannot escape being affected by these reference groups ranging from Manchester United to the City Bank, from Harvard to the BBC World Service. This leads to immense enthusiasm, and this enthusiasm is seen in new things happening all around us: Indian television coming of age, proliferation 24-hour news channels, remarkable growth in the music industry, Bollywood becoming increasingly transnational and multi-ethnic, banks with computers and ATM facilities, children feeling more and more comfortable with the internet, and our universities collaborating with the other international institutions. It is a world filled with immense vitality, mobility and communication. There is indeed a thrill in a world in which one learns *Bharatanatyam*, reads African poetry, watches BBC news, and sends e-mail messages to one's friends in Australia!

In fact, this cultural diffusion which is implicit in the globalizing process can lead to a more mature cross-cultural understanding. It should not be forgotten that we often feel tempted to generate stereotypes about other cultures, and these stereotypes have by no means elevated our conscience. Instead, we have experienced hatred and mistrust. But if globalization succeeds in fighting these stereotypes through more sustained interaction among cultures, it is likely to consolidate the ethos of true interculturalism. And it has really begun to happen. There is every reason to feel happy when we see the increasing popularity of Indian/Chinese cuisine in the West, or to take yet another example, Madona using the Vedic symbol in her album. And it is also a sign of the changing times that Hollywood attempts to employ mixed, multinational casts of actors and actresses and varieties of local settings. Indeed, these cross-cultural plots of music, clothing, behaviour, advertising, theatre, body language and visual communication are everywhere—say, the way films like *Bollywood-Hollywood, American Deshi, Bend it Like Bekham* and *Mitra My Friend* have made their presence felt in India. Not solely that. Even in serious intellectual endeavours we see how cultural boundaries become increasingly fuzzy. Jhumpa Lahiri writes about the NRI children in America, and Gyatri Chakravarti Spivak sees beyond Derrida, and popularizes Mahesweta Devi in Euro-American universities. And even an unknown teacher like me—in the process of interacting with students from Iran, Sri Lanka, Kenya, Japan, Finland and Australia in a multicultural class room in the Jawaharlal Nehru University—experiences the beauty of this globalizing process, and its ethos of cultural diffusion. Possibly these students overcome many stereotypes about India. India, they begin to realize, is not just a land of poverty, hunger, and superstitions; India is also a possibility filled with critical discourses and political vibrancy. Likewise, I alter my stereotypes about them. My Iranian student becomes a family friend; I see him as a humane, critical, alert thinker—not a typical 'Islamic' fundamentalist' the Ayatolla Khomenis of the world remind us of. Or, when a student from Finland begins to communicate with me in Hindi, I do realize that the 'West' is not just a colonial stereotype; people in the West are also like us: humane, vulnerable and ambiguous. In other words, as cultures interact more steadily and rapidly, it becomes possible for all of us to rediscover our shared humanity: unity amidst differences.

True, this global cultural exchange does not approve of a 'puritan' notion of culture. Instead, there are experimentations, hybridization and new forms of synthesis. It is a fluid process leading to a refreshing change from the old-fashioned, static, closed, orthodox mind-set.

So when my daughter—a school girl—tells me about *Bryan Adams, Britney Spears* or *Backstreet Boys*, I see the beauty of this process: how the mind is evolving, growing and transcending territorial boundaries. It is also important to acknowledge that globalization does not necessarily deny cultural memory. Instead, as we see, local/national cultures, far from withering away, continue to survive and innovate (Appadurai, 1990). It is because culture is not like technology. Old technologies can be replaced by new ones. Cultures, however, last longer than technologies. Unlike science/technology, cultures do not follow a straightforward/linear path. In the domain of culture 'old' and 'new' often co-exist. Let me give an example. The other day I attended a wedding ceremony in a posh South Delhi colony. The boy was a Punjabi, but settled in Romania. The girl was a Maithili Brahmin; she was brought up in Bangalore, and had just got a job in America. They were in love, and they were getting married in Delhi. The entire phenomenon reminded me of what the proponents of globalization would have regarded as 'time-space compression'. Yes, Delhi, Bangalore, Punjab, Romania and America seemed to have combined together to constitute a 'global village'. But then, this globalization, as I noticed with immense joy, could not negate cultural memories. The priest, the Vedic hymns, and the Maithili songs sung by old ladies representing the girl's family conveyed a very strong message: cultures would not accept their defeat so easily. Not solely that. Cultures too have the power to innovate and survive. Yes, even in this global village we do experience the aliveness of local/regional/national cultures. It is, therefore, not surprising that I often come across many students (who are otherwise global and mobile) learning *Bharatanatyam* and classical music; Ravi Shankar, Bhimsen Joshi and Mallika Sarabhai, as the success story of the SPICMACAY programmes suggest, continue to have an appeal among the younger generation; shopping malls and supermarkets have not been able to destroy the charm of rural meals and local bazaars, and Pepsi, Pizza and Hamburger are not yet powerful enough to deprive us of our taste for *lassi, samosa* and *jalebi*!

In this context, it is important to realize that we are not necessarily passive/empty receivers of cultural products and practices. We all have our specific histories, cultural memories and local contexts. This entire socio-existential domain that constitutes our biographies does have a definite impact on the way we receive, interpret and relate to cultural products and practices. Hence even if there is something called a packaged global culture emanating from the dominant centres of the world, the process of reception can become contextual and hermeneutic (Thompson, 1995: 40). In other words, there is a possibility of a localized appropriation of global culture. This perhaps reduces the possibility of cultural imperialism. Yes, we do have the power to reinteret, modulate, and even alter the global cultural products. This seems to be the reason why, as many media experts have begun to argue, Shakekespeare no longer belongs to England; he has been subject to a wide-ranging cultural interpretation and staging. Indeed, there are innumerable illustrations to show how we have localized and contextualized global products—say, a classical film like *Sound and Music* having a distinctively Indian flavour in Hindi and Bengali, or Coke, as the famous Amir Khan ad suggests, using multiple ethnic/regional symbols to popularize itself as *'Thande Matlab Coca-Cola'*. This means that be it film, music or any other cultural product, the local is not altogether dead. Instead of a thoroughly homogenized culture, a creative/complex interplay of the global and the local is possibly taking place.

IV
Fractured Global Culture: Asymmetry and Discontents

While I acknowledge these creative possibilities inherent in the process of globalization, I also sense its discontents. True, a close look at the emerging *popular culture*—video music, television serials, dietary practice and dress pattern—does indicate the process of widespread cultural diffusion and hybridity. In fact, in these cultural products we see how territorial boundaries become obsolete, and a new notion of aesthetics emerges. There is no denying the fact that this entire process has created immense enthusiasm, particularly among the urban younger generation. The success stories of television programmes like *Indian Idol* suggest how young talents are overcoming all barriers, and making their presence felt in the domain of popular culture. Everywhere around us we are noticing tremendous enthusiasm with *hybridity*—a group of young girls (the much talked about group called *Viva*) singing Hindi songs in a thoroughly Americanized style on the MTV channel, FM radio channels repeatedly 'experimenting' with the style/grammar of Hindi, and McDonald's emerging as an important site for birthday parties, even for supposedly conservative Hindu families! Yet, I cannot escape my deep ambiguity, because I also doubt the depth and rigour of these cultural products. Let me state my reasons.

To begin with, what comes to my mind is the way it seeks to nurture a consciousness that is oriented to pleasure: pleasure in unlimited consumption of goods—material as well as symbolic. Indeed, globalization as it exists is impossible to imagine without this consumptionist/pleasure-seeking/mass culture—the culture which promotes what Erich Fromm once regarded as a 'having mode of existence' (Fromm, 1982). The site of this culture can be anything: from the MTV channel to the nearest shopping mall. Everything is commodified, and available in abundance—food, sex, health and vitality. And we are just required to have it more and more. Likewise, it promotes the logic of the market. Everything can be dislocated from its specific context. It can be seen in the way even culture-specific qualitative experiences—from ethnic music to environmental movements—are now appropriated and 'protected' through international funding. It has indeed a disruptive influence on the cultural landscape. Yogendra Singh has rightly pointed out:

> It tends to become more alluring as it offers to the traditional artists enormous profit and publicity for their consent to be incorporated after having destroyed their traditional social base. Popular culture alienates not only the artist from his art forms but also art from its organic link with the community. It abstracts culture for the media of work, fractures its aesthetic expressiveness, and destroys the dialectic of its sacred-secular worldview (Singh, 2000:111).

Indeed, a culture of this kind speeds up what can be regarded as 'sponsorship' culture. Pepsi/Coke promoting Indian cricket, the international fashion market celebrating Indian femininity, and transnational corporations promoting Durga puja in Kolkata and Delhi reveal the point I am referring to. Culture, because of the excessive burden of sponsorship, loses its authenticity: its organic link with our shared memory. Furthermore, it technologizes every sphere of cultural creation. An example that I find strikingly revealing is the Michael Jackson phenomenon. As a matter of fact, Jackson is the creation of the technologized global culture. He symbolizes that music is no longer music; it is a piece of technological spectacle as gorgeous as man's journey into space. Jackson conveys a message: even man's most intimate moments of joy and sorrow can no longer be experienced in their profound simplicity. Music becomes a technological spectacle.

> The spectacle presents itself as something enormously positive, indisputable and inaccessible. It says nothing more than 'that which appears is good, that which is good appears'. The attitude which it demands in principle is passive acceptance which in fact it already obtained by its manner of appearing without reply, by its monopoly of appearance (Debord, 2001: 141).

Indeed, everything becomes a spectacle: television music, shopping mall, war, and even love on the eve of Valentine's Day. Not surprisingly, we find ourselves amidst a culture that tends to promote instantaneity and temporality. It is like negating heritage, memory and continuity. What prevails is the media-induced, market-oriented, technologized spectacular show in which images and icons are perpetually created and forgotten, or, to borrow Fredrich Jamenson's words, it is a 'new kind of flatness or depthlessness, a new kind of superficiality' (Jameson, 1984: 53–92).

This critique of global popular culture, I am aware, can be alleged as elitist: an intellectual endeavour to undermine people's tastes and choices. And postmodernists may find some kind of moral puritanism in my discourse. My intention, as I have already stated, is not to suggest that everything about this culture is hollow and superficial. There are indeed experimentations; there is a spirit of innovation, and as the proliferation of the culture industry suggests, more and more talents are coming in the domain of popular culture. But the overall trend that I see in the emergent global culture, I must admit, is problematic. It doesn't seem to have the depth and rigour of, to take a specific illustration, the classical Indian art. I am often reminded of the aesthetic sensibility that Anand K. Coomaraswamy talked about (Coomaraswamy, 1982: 102–114). Take, for instance, Indian music. 'The dominant subject matter of the songs', said Coomaraswamy, 'is human or divine love in all its aspects, or the direct praise of God, and the words are always sincere and passionate' (Ibid: 108). Or, how do we understand that in the musical form called *alap* only meaningless syllables are used? The fact is that 'the song is more than the words of the song' (Ibid: 110); the words exist only to express a mood rather than tell any story. The Indian music, wrote Coomaraswamy, 'reflects an emotion and an experience which are deeper and wider and older than the emotion or wisdom of any single individual. Its sorrow is without tears, its joy without exultation and it is passionate without any loss of serenity' (Ibid: 111). Possibly this depth is missing in a large segment of contemporary cultural products. It is more about colourful packaging—about gorgeous technology, about decorative style, about words without coherence, about desire, and about restlessness. The experience I gain while listening to Bhimsen Joshi, or reading Tagore's *Geetanjali*, I know, would seldom be found in the cultural goods that bombard me every day: MTV spectacles, Hollywood blockbusters and television soap operas. Again, these products are not like immensely vital folk forms. Because in folk arts one experiences an organic link with the local milieu, its hopes and sorrows, and a sense of unity between the entertainer and the consumer. Instead, these global products are now manufactured, packaged, mass-circulated—like any other commodity in the market place. It seeks to create a mind-set: depoliticized, pleasure-seeking, money-oriented, and devoid of cultural memory.

Yes, I am willing to admit that it would be wrong to say that globalization is only about the globalization of American mass culture. It would indeed be wrong to say that there is nothing in the cultural domain beyond MTV and McDonald's. As I have already indicated, there is a possibility of the diffusion of classical or emancipatory art forms and ideas. But then, the market is so overwhelmingly powerful that radical ideas and creations are often overshadowed by the continual flow of sleek/popularized/

mass culture. Even in the world characterized by communication revolution, our children, it has to be admitted, know less about Herman Hease and Jean Paul Sartre, but more about Hollywood and Michael Jackson. And this globalized standardized culture, I am trying to indicate, does not necessarily do justice to our finer aesthetic sensibility that strives for peace and calmness: the poetry and metaphysics to establish a link between the temporal and the transcendental, and the sensual and the spiritual. My intention is not to romanticize India by arguing that Indian culture does necessarily always have that depth. My point is simple and straight. The packaged global mass culture violates the aesthetic sensibility of humanity as such. Because it is essentially about pleasure, packaging, commodification and sensation. The danger is that it insults the depth that sustains our humanity: the depth that we see in the *Upanishadic* prayer, in the *Sermon on the Mount*, in Dostoyvesky's novels, in the poetry of William Blake, in the ecstasy of Sufi poetry, in Krishna's transcendental dance with the *gopis*, in the music of Beethoven and Mozart, and in the beauty of folk arts and handicrafts.

There is yet another problem—the problem of asymmetry. Not all cultures/nations exist as equal partners in the globalizing process. In fact, the most important economic, political and cultural-ideological goods that circulate around the globe tend to be owned and/or controlled by small groups in a relatively small number of countries' (Sklair, 1991: 6). It is not surprising. Because many of the largest TNCs have assets and annual sales far in excess of the GNP of about half of the countries of the world. For example, in 1986, according to the world Bank, 64 out of 120 countries had a GNP of less than $ 10 billion. And during the same period the annual sales of the McDonald's fast food corporation was $ 124 billion. In such a scenario the exchange of cultures remains inherently inequal. Thailand, Argentina, Nigeria—in fact, the majority of developing countries are exposed to the media messages emanating from these corporations. Indeed, these enterprises are organized through globally integrated networks. Even when there is limited adaptation to local circumstances as with McDonald's in east Asia, the global network in the end wins out. It is in this context that Urry, I think, has made an interesting observation:

> The Managing Director of McDonald's in Singapore explains as follows: 'McDonald's sells... a system, not products. This 'system' is taught at Hamburger university and systematized in the 600-page *Operations and Training Manual*. Certain key features of the global network include not only standardized products but also the standardized and monitored 'smiling service' to strangers. Such globally integrated networks produce not only predictable material goods and services, but also calculable and controllable simulations of experiences apparently 'more real than the original' (Urry, 2003: 57–58.)

As a matter of fact, the overwhelming presence of the cultural package that these transnational corporations manufacture causes deep asymmetry in the exchange of cultures. In a way, the exchange of cultures cannot be separated from the discourse of power. Not all cultures, not all voices get an equal opportunity to become an active component of the globalization process. Where is, for instance, Sri Lanka or Bangladesh or Kenya in this cultural diffusion? As a matter of fact, the balance between US/ foreign and domestic origin mass media communication in key areas is skewed towards the former, and Third World origin mass media messages seldom get respectable exposure in the United States or other developed countries. Look at the globalization of popular music. The fact is that the 'global' music industry remains remarkably concentrated both in terms of control and sales. It is 'defined by the North Atlantic Anglo-American cultural movements of sounds and images and European, American and Japanese dominance of financial capital and hardware' (Negus, 1992: 14). Because of this cultural imbalance we know more about American popular culture, Hollywood films, Western music and BBC-CNN news package; but seldom do we show the similar interest in the cultural matrix of, say, Bangladesh, Sri Lanka and Kenya. In fact, it is *asymmetrical globalization*; the dominant centres of the global power often decide the nature and mode of cultural exchange. The question is: what is our position in this entire process? Well, it is often said that India as an old civilization possesses a rich cultural tradition, and it has made its presence felt all over the world. True, we do not just receive cultural products from the West. We too contribute and influence the world. But then, this 'Indianness', as many would argue, has already been typified and packaged as 'spirituality'. The assumption is that we import science, technology, Pizza and Michael Jackson; and we export 'spirituality'. In fact, the process of exporting spirituality is quite old. One can, for instance, refer to Swami Vivekananda's celebrated address in the Chicago religious conference in 1893: the way the charismatic saint made Hinduism popular among 'the sisters and brothers of America'. Possibly the process continues even today. From the phenomenon called ISKCON to the cult of Bhagwan Rajneesh and Mahesh Yogi—Hinduism was often packaged in a fashion that made India saleable. This process further reinforced the image of 'spiritual' India: an 'old' civilization providing a kind of parapsychology—a way of getting away from the suffocating behaviourism and materialistic metaphysics of the West (Matilal, 2002). But then, what needs to be understood is that this duality—Western materialism vs. Indian spiritualism—is essentially hierarchical and problematic. In this cultural politics the hidden assumption is that in the real practical world that matters, we are nothing. We need to depend on the West for its science, technology, commerce and trade. And if some 'sensitive' souls of the West get tired of its gross materialism, they may come to India for 'spiritual tourism', stay at Haridwar and Rishikesh, and take a series of courses on the *Bhagvadgita*. Possibly things are changing now. IITs are becoming 'brand names' in America, information technology is often associated with India, Bollywood has emerged as the only feasible competitor of Hollywood, and Indian diaspora is fast becoming a force to reckon with. While these changes do suggest a new beginning, a lot has to be done to resist the 'essentialization' of India, and bring about true equality in the domain of cultural exchange.

As things stand, it is, however, futile to pretend that we all are equal in this global village. I wish to make sense of this asymmetry through my own experience in the domain of academic culture. What I witness is an extremely narrow and restricted notion of the world. It would not be wrong to say that the USA, England, Australia, France and Germany constitute the small world in which students/researchers/professors seek to move around. I have not yet come across a researcher/teacher expressing his/her willingness to visit, say, a university in Bangladesh, Kenya and Sri Lanka. Nor do I see a professor from Oxford or Harvard coming to Indian universities on sabbatical. Not solely that. Seldom do we establish an organic link with local/regional/and even South Asian universities. Recently, my department has started collaborating with a leading European university. As a joint venture, it has offered a course on global studies. This has generated tremendous momentum in the university. Yet, what I notice with sadness and despair is that no such effort is being made on our part—a leading metropolitan university—to have a similar kind of collaboration with, say, a university in Ujjain, Bhopal or Kathmandu. While we move towards the West, regional disparities continue to prevail and multiply. As a matter of fact, Euro-American universities, for all practical purposes, have become the dominant partners in this academic exchange. They have the funds—the infrastructure to seduce us. The results are disastrous: largescale migration of students/teachers from India to the West, the continual flow of books, journals, discourses and academic fashions from the West, and our pathetic dependence on these borrowed ideas. This one-way traffic has by no means enriched our universities. We have lost many finer minds, good scientists and intellectuals. With more and more globalization we see the growing decline in the culture of Indian universities, we see the entry of foreign universities, and the increasing craze for foreign degrees and diplomas. This is certainly not a good thing for a civilization that seeks to retain its self-confidence.

V
Cultural Anguish and Misdirected Rebellions

Globalization, as I have indicated, has diverse possibilities. It cannot be condemned as just Americanization or cultural imperialism. Its positive potential—its ability to generate a cross-cultural conversation and an open/fluid/inclusive culture—has to be acknowledged. It is, however, equally true that this positive potential cannot be fully unfolded unless we resist the asymmetry of globalization. And this asymmetry is rooted in the dynamics of contemporary history: the overwhelming presence of global capitalism, the steady retreat of the nation-state from the domain of social sectors, and the growing helplessness of developing countries to have any control on the ongoing flow of media-inducted/market-oriented cultural commodities and symbols. But then, whenever there is asymmetry and inequality, there is bound to be resistance. If the existing form of globalization further hierarchizes the world, weakens developing countries, and insults their cultures, it is quite likely that the dissenting voice would emerge; globalization would be critiqued and resisted. Yet, it is important to realize that not all sorts of resistance necessarily take us to a better world. Because rebellions, as history has demonstrated, may degenerate into militant conservatism or savage/barbaric acts of violence. We, therefore, need to be cautious. It is in this context that I wish to speak of three such *misdirected rebellions* which we should be careful about.

First, what we are witnessing all around is *terrorist violence*. In recent times, as the 9/11 incident demonstrates, it has shown a high degree of hostility towards the US-centric global project. It is feared that the US-led world—with its gigantic techno-military power, its expansionist media empire and its mass culture of consumerism—is invading the 'sacred' domain of other cultures. This fear, largely real, and partly exaggerated has intensified cultural anxiety and insecurity. Furthermore, the recent war, be it in Afghanistan or in Iraq, has caused widespread resentment and anxiety. Why should one accept the USA as the self-proclaimed moral guardian for the rest of the world? Or, why should one say 'yes' to its 'civilizing mission' to rescue a 'medieval' Afghanistan or a 'tyrannical' Iraq, and impose its discourses of 'liberal democracy and human rights'? (Tibi, 2004: 335–39). In fact, terrorism emerges out of this anguish. It reveals the wounded ego caused by sustained humiliation. It is nothing but the manifestation of this hidden anger. It is the desperate urge to terrorize the enemy. In a way, it is a sado-masochistic response to an unjust world in which the arrogance of the privileged few leads the rest to internalize the language of envy, jealousy, hatred and violence. But then, terrorism, it has to be realized, is self-defeating, because it reproduces itself. No wonder, we are also witnessing counter terrorism—this time by America, its army and media, the way it mythologizes its victory, its 'war against terror' through television spectacles, the way it bombards our minds by images of a defeated/ disoriented Saddam Hussain or a medieval Afghanistan filled with the Taliban brand of darkness, and the way, as Noam Chomsky lamented, a culture is created in which 'only violent thugs relish the role of 'enforcer', and delight in sending their military forces and goon squads to torture and kill people who are too weak too fight back' (Chomsky, 1989: 262). Indeed, we get caught into a vicious circle: George Bush, his arrogance, his stubbornness, the way he projects the other as 'evil', and then the mindlessness of an Osama Bin Laden or a Saddam Hussain. There seems to be no escape from the language of hatred, mistrust and exclusion.

Possibly this conflict has led many like Samuel Huntington to speak of the 'clash of civilizations' which has generated all sorts of dualistic stereotypes. With the Islamic Resurgence, as Huntington believes, the West is being seen as 'arrogant, materialistic, repressive, brutal and decadent'. And, for the West, the 'Islamic threat' appears to be real; Islam is seen as a 'source of nuclear proliferation, terrorism and unwanted migrants'. As the West declares a war against these Islamic 'rougue/terrorist 'states, the 'civilizational conflict' becomes more obvious and acute (Huntington, 1996). For Huntington, in our times the most pervasive, important and dangerous conflicts will be between peoples belonging to different cultures. The West too, as he feels, has to realize that there are limits to the universality of its cultural mission because 'it is false, it is immoral, and it is dangerous' (Ibid: 310). The message he seeks to convey is that there are diverse cultures and civilizations, and conflict is almost inevitable. Yet, we would argue that the asymmetry of globalization can by no means be combated by the 'clash of civilizations' which manifests itself in the worldwide terrorist violence. Even if this clash appears 'real', we need to overcome its nihilism, and strive for a dialogic world. Even the proponent of the 'clash of civilizations' thesis would concede that 'the futures of both peace and civilization depend upon understanding and cooperation among the political, spiritual, and intellectual leaders of the world's major civilizations' (Ibid: 321).

Second, the fear of cultural invasion may lead to a counter-tendency: the reinvention/reconstruction of the 'past glory', or the mythologization of the old tradition. This is like promoting a regressive trend: there is nothing worth-learning in all that is happening around us; go back to the past, and salvage yourself! This sort of puritanism or conservatism is also a source of violence: *fundamentalist violence* against innovation, creativity and social transformation. The danger is that while evolving a critique of globalization, puritan/conservative forces often end up promoting the oppressive elements in the culture which they seek to protect. I wish to give a simple example to make my point. There is every reason to be unhappy with, say, the phenomenon called 'beauty contest': a global cultural spectacle that imposes a marketized/standardized notion of beauty on diverse traditions. Yet, this critique does by no means suggest that, as anyone with gender sensitivity would concede, the position of a woman in, say, a traditional/patriarchal/Brahminical culture is worth preserving. The glamorous/gorgeous woman we see in the beauty contest is a product of the culture of mass consumerism; she has already been reduced into an object of male gaze, a visual pleasure and a site of unbounded desire. But then, the perception of a woman we see in, say, the *Manusmriti*—'In childhood a female must be subject to her father, in youth to her husband, when her lord is dead, to her sons; a woman must never be independent' (Manusmriti V: 148)—can by no means be regarded as a better alternative. It is, therefore, not surprising that the assertion of fundamentalism/puritanism has always been perceived as a threat to some of the egalitarian ideals like gender equality and justice. As fundamentalism emerges in diverse forms—from Islamic terrorism to Hindu nationalism—in different parts of the world, it is important to be careful about it. It is in this context that I wish to recall Benjamin Barber's brilliant observations (Barber, 2004: 29–35). Barber reminds us of the danger implicit in the emergent McWorld which 'mesmerizes people everywhere with fast music, fast computers, and fast food—MTV, Macintosh, and McDonald's—pressing nations into one homogeneous global theme park' (Ibid: 29). But then, argues Barber, Jihad can by no means prove itself as a meaningful alternative:

> Jihad and McWorld operate with equal strength in opposite directions, the one driven by parochial hatreds, the other by universalizing markets, the one re-creating ancient sub-national and ethnic borders from within, the other making national borders porous from without. Yet, Jihad and McWorld have this in common: they both make war on the sovereign nation-state and thus undermine the nation-state's democratic institutions. Each eschews civil society and belittles democratic citizenship, neither seeks alternative democratic institutions. Their common thread is indifference to civil liberty (Ibid: 31).

Yes, globalization cannot and should not be fought by an orthodox/puritan/conservative mind-set. What is, therefore, desirable is to retain a dialogic/innovative spirit, resist any kind of ethnocentrism, and learn, whenever necessary, from the other cultures, and enrich our horizon. I agree with Bimal Krishna Matilal when he reflects on the dynamics of cultural interaction:

> The utterly ethnocentric person cannot even make the first move to comprehend that there are 'other worlds' much like the celebrated frog (in the Indian parable of the Frog and the Well) who, living all his life in the well never comprehended that there was a world

> outside...The first significant step to overcome such ethnocentrism is not only to recognize that there are others but also to comprehend that their beliefs and acts may to some extent be incommensurable with ours. But then they may also be, under certain circumstances, real options for us (Matilal, 1988: 35).

Third, the fear of globalization may promote the doctrine of *militant nationalism*. Protect the nation. Sanctify it. Preserve its culture, and its boundaries. And suspect your potential enemies! Yes, this sort of nationalism has an immensely emotive appeal. It gives us a cause, an identity to feel proud of, and an agenda to accomplish. The heightened awareness of the modern nation as a political collective, it could be argued, did help us to overcome internal differences, and consolidate an united front to fight against colonialism. Furthermore, the sovereign nation-state, provided it is not indifferent to the doctrine of collective welfare, can indeed play an important role in bringing about equality and symmetry in the world. But then, as history has revealed time and again, the emancipatory possibilities of the nation may be overshadowed by the cult of aggressive nationalism. In this context I wish to recall Tagore who warned us of its discontents (Tagore, 1985). He felt that nationalism had become a 'great menace'. As Tagore realized, the narcissism of the modern nation, its 'iron chains of organization', its inflated ego, and hence its perpetual insecurity could be seen in the devastating war and all-pervasive violence. Who could deny these pathologies of nationalism—authoritarianism, fascism, and imperialism that shocked the West and the rest of the world in the twentieth century? This sort of nationalism, for Tagore, was against the humanistic ethos of civilization; it was essentially life-negating.

> Nation is like the difference between the handloom and

> the power loom. In the products of the handloom the magic of man's living-fingers finds its expression, and its hum harmonizes with the music of life. But the power loom is relentlessly lifeless and accurate and monotonous in its production (Ibid: 10).

India, the poet asserted, should learn from its history, and resist this sort of nationalism. It should derive its inspiration from its civilizational ideal which is to work for 'an adjustment of races, to acknowledge the real differences between them, and yet seek some basis of unity' (Ibid: 59). As a matter of fact, Tagore was not wrong in apprehending the danger: a mind that worships the 'fetish of nationalism', and refuses to open up becomes exclusivist, violent and anxiety-ridden. No wonder, the cult of militant nationalism cannot be separated from the institutionalized violence-massive growth of techno-military industry, cultural hysteria, and the projection of the 'other' as one's potential enemy. Asymmetrical globalization or its implicit hegemonic urge is indeed bad. But then, militant nationalism, far from being a meaningful answer, is the other side of the same coin. It cannot fight the culture of exclusion. Instead, it seeks to replace one kind of domination/hegemony by another. How can it then combat what is often regarded as 'imperialistic' globalization? With his poetic sensitivity, his expanded horizon, and his openness, Tagore celebrated a kind of universalism which, as Ashis Nandy argued, 'endorsed a large, plural concept of India' (Nandy, 1994). Yes, life is growth, and we require innovation and openness, not a retreat into a closed world of narcissistic nationalism. The spirit of Tagore's universal humanism we must recall as we respond to globalization.

VI
Art of Resistance: Towards Symmetrical Globalization

The prevalent practice of globalization—with its inherent

asymmetry and hierarchy---is bound to arouse dissent. Not all forms of dissent are, however, desirable. It is in this context that I wish to speak of the *art of resistance*. Yes, I insist, it is an art. Because a true rebel, like an artist, is immensely subtle, creative and humane. Far from being merely angry and reactive, she makes a significant difference, and through alternative practices portrays the landscape of a new world. Her rebellion does not, therefore, cause hatred. Nor is it merely instrumental which is based on the cold logic of strategic diplomacy. Instead, it is insightful; it is filled with a vision; it is enriched by the philosophic wisdom of revolutionaries like Marx and Gandhi, the aesthetic sensibility of cultural creators like Tolstoy and Tagore, and the profound universalism of spiritual revelations like the *Upanishads*. Like an artist, a true rebel invites all—even those she is revolting against—to the domain of her creation. This art of resistance—provided we succeed in internalizing it—would give us tremendous creativity to engage with the changing cultural landscape, and replace the asymmetrical globalization with a more humane, egalitarian and symmetrical one. That would be our contribution to the making of a new world.

Let us begin with *dialogue* as a mode of cultural practice. Dialogue means a sense of humility and humbleness, not the denial of self-dignity. Dialogue is essentially reciprocity; the willingness to learn from others, and at the same time the courage to stand up and resist all sorts of hegemony and domination. It is in this sense that dialogue is different from colonial arrogance—the desire to dominate others, and hierarchize the world. Dialogue is different from ethnocentrism: the belief that one's own culture alone is supreme, and everything else is insignificant. Dialogue is indeed an experience of the 'fusion of horizons'. Edward Said captured this spirit when he wrote:

> Survival in fact is about the connections between things; in Eliot's phrase, reality cannot be deprived of the 'other

> echoes (that) inhabit the garden'. It is more rewarding—and more difficult—to think concretely and sympathetically, contrapuntally, about others than only about 'us'. But this also means not trying to rule others, not trying to classify them or put them in hierarchies, above all, not constantly reiterating how 'our' culture is number one (or not number one for that matter) (Said, 1994:408).

It is this spirit of dialogue that we need to renew in order to resist asymmetrical globalization as well as cultural puritanism. And I would argue that 'Indianness' itself is an experience of dialogue, because Indianness can by no means be equated with one particular culture—say, the Vedic Hindu culture. As an evolving process it has been perpetually growing; multiple traditions emanating from diverse religions and ethnic/linguistic communities enrich it, and evolve a notion of *civilizational unity* that, far from being oppressive and hegemonic, is essentially accommodative and inclusive. As a matter of fact, the continual interplay of classical and folk traditions fascinates the sociologists working on Indian culture. Yes, what distinguishes India is the enormous plurality of cultural patterns and styles at the local and regional levels. It would not be an exaggeration to say that the cultural situation in India varies every few miles, and even within a single village each caste has a culture which is somewhat different from that of the other. Yet, 'there has existed a continued dialogue and interaction or even creative synthesis between the "great traditions" or elite culture and that of the "little traditions" or the culture of the folk or local communities' (Singh, 2000:79).

It was this dialogic spirit that, as Abid Husain would have argued, led the 'national culture' to grow, and to enrich itself from the creative voices emanating from Buddhism and Jainism, from the heritage of the Islamic culture, and from the spirit of political democracy and industrial progress rooted in the culture of Western modernity (Husain, 1985: 161–75). Indeed, this cultural syncretism has been reflected in the ideals and practices that sought to enrich our civilization. Kabir refuted all sorts of orthodoxy and exclusion, Ramakrishna—a devotee of Goddess Kali—didn't hesitate to engage with the other religious traditions; Gandhi could retain the courage to visit Noakhali, and radiate the message of love and harmony even at a time when there was widespread communal violence, cultural exclusion and hatred; Tagore (inspired by the *Upanishadic* ideal of universality) established an *ashram* that invited the seekers of truth from all over the world, and ordinary people—Hindus and Muslims alike—didn't have much difficulty in relating to Mother Teresa, and her immense faith in the Christian message of love and service. It is this dialogic capacity—not paranoia and insecurity—that should be seen as our strength: something we need to resist the ongoing process of one-dimensional globalization as well as the fundamentalist politics of cultural exclusion. It is dialogue and dialogue alone that would enable us to experiment and innovate; these experimentations, unlike the prevalent global culture industry characterized by instantaneity and temporality, are likely to add depth to our creations—the depth that we experience when, to take a couple of examples, Satyajit Ray used modern cinema to portray the classic narrative of rural Bengal, or Ravishankar arrived at the fusion of musical traditions, and became truly global. At a time when the thesis of the 'clash of civilizations' is gaining popularity, we must tell the world about our strength, and our ability to think of 'dialogue among civilizations'. Indeed, we can stand up if we learn from this dialogic spirit, engage meaningfully with the rest of the world, and think of an India that is truly cosmopolitan, yet having a sense of continuity and rich cultural memory.

It is at this juncture that the meaning of patriotism needs

to be redefined. Patriotism, I have already indicated, may degenerate into aggressive/militant nationalism which is by no means conducive to the growth of an egalitarian/harmonic world. Because symmetrical globalization requires a mature cross-cultural understanding, a genuine concern for our shared humanity, not narrow/narcissistic nationalist pride. Likewise, patriotism, as we have often noticed in our times, can also degenerate into a mere sentimental outburst. It is like feeling excited only when India wins the Kargil war, or defeats Pakistan in cricket, while remaining callous, dishonest and indifferent to people in everyday life. In the new world we are striving for there should not be any space for this sort of patriotism. Yet, it is equally important to realize that in the name of 'global concerns' one should not remain indifferent to the local milieu, its needs and aspirations. In the prevalent mode of globalization, as we have seen, not all partners are equal. That is why, to deny the concerns of the local culture or the marginalized groups is to serve only the privileged ones. We, therefore, need to reconcile the local and the global, patriotism and cosmopolitanism. It is an exceedingly subtle endeavour—an art of living—that needs to be understood. I wish to give an example from my own field: the domain of knowledge. Yes, the search for knowledge, and commitment to it transcends all barriers and borders. That is why, it can be said that an Indian scientist working in an American university is serving science itself, and hence the entire humankind. It would indeed be absurd to condemn him as someone who has betrayed his nation. Great minds, we are told, have no nationalist/local colour. It is wrong to monopolize Albert Einstein, Salman Rushdie or Amartya Sen. Yet, this does by no means suggest that every 'non-resident Indian' scholar is like these illustrious figures. As a matter of fact, it is often the desire for immediate success, wealth and technological comforts that leads many—scientists, doctors, engineers and other professionals—to leave the country. America or Australia or Canada becomes a 'dream land' that seduces them. And herein lies the real problem. To equate every IIT product settling down in America with a selfless love of humankind is to devalue the true spirit of cosmopolitanism. Because this sort of 'brain drain'—no matter how justified in the name of professional reasons—disregards the local community that needs, and needs urgently, the service of its doctors, engineers and scientists. As we have already seen, it is still an unequal world, and serving only the privileged nations does not end this asymmetry. What is, therefore, needed is an added concern for those who need to rise up, and cultivate their resources to create a truly just world. India, therefore, needs the service of its scientists, knowledge-seekers and professionals. Yes, to stay in India and work here is by no means an easy task. It means enormous difficulties and of course, huge monetary loss. Yet, the challenge is to do it despite all odds. This is what I wish to regard as the test of true patriotism. It is the kind of patriotism that could be seen when, to take a couple of illustrations, Satyajit Ray, instead of going to Hollywood, made films in Kolkata in Bengali, or when M.N. Srinivas, instead of teaching abroad, created institutions in India for promoting sociological research. And the patriotism of this kind, I insist, is not an act of indifference to the rest of the world. Nor is it a doctrine of militant nationalism. Its only objective is to create a just world, and humanize it. Globalization should not mean indifference to one's own surroundings. Serving one's immediate/local milieu can well be the beginning of serving the larger world. That is, I guess, the spirit of real cosmopolitanism. It is indeed nice to see this quest even in a popular film like Ashutosh Gowarinkar's *Swadesh*. The film depicts—and depicts with immense sensitivity—the journey of an Indian scientist working with the NASA. It is a journey from the metropolis to the periphery, from privilege to hardship. That is why, it is a journey that invites challenges. The scientist comes back to India, experiences enormous difficulties emanating from the specificity of local problems. And finally, he decides to work in India; he accepts the new challenge. The film does not romanticize India. Nor does it condemn the West. Instead, the film wants us to acknowledge the need to address our own specific problems. The film is about a reverse journey: not from the periphery to the centre for privilege and comfort, but from the centre to the periphery with complete awareness of the difficulties and challenges ahead. Let it be yet another meaningful story of globalization.

And finally, it has to be realized that the art of resistance remains incomplete without an alternative mode of living. It is qualitatively different from the pleasure-seeking, consumptionist lifestyle. It is to realize happiness in harmony, richness in austerity, and power in simplicity. It is this mode of living that can inspire one to resist the mythology of global capitalism, and its notion of 'good living'. We should not forget that the prevalent form of asymmetrical globalization rests on the power of wealth. It is this power manifesting itself in the techno-military might that privileges a few nations, and makes others subdued, helpless and pathetically dependent. It is the principle that nothing succeeds like material power—the power of the market—that globalizes itself, and causes widespread cultural disturbance:

> ...the 'new' capitalism mobilized all its resources to promote in the individual a profound sense of insufficiency which could only be relieved, and then only temporarily, in the act of consumption... Accelerated production could only deliver greater profits and growth if it were matched by accelerated consumption. For some products, this could be achieved by increasing the pace of product deterioration, thus shortening replacement time; but for most products and services it could only be brought about by engendering

> a perpetual sate of dissatisfaction in the psyche of the consumer. The gratification yielded by one consumption experience had to give way in the shortest possible time to the desire for another. Indeed, the ideal consumer would forego satisfaction altogether—and desire only desire (Bennett, 2001:161).

It is obvious that this sort of global capitalism cannot be fought merely through altered cultural practices. It needs serious intervention in the domain of political economy. But then, no struggle is merely an economic struggle; culture, as I have said, is equally an important site of resistance. That is why, the alternative mode of living I am talking about is bound to generate new confidence: the ability to assert, and realize that there is a world beyond global capitalism and its seductive consumerism. I often recall the *Brhad-aranyaka Upanishad*. Yajnavalkya offers to divide all his earthly possessions between his two wives, Katyani and Maitreyi. The latter asks whether the whole world filled with wealth can give her life eternal. Yajnavalkya replies: 'No, your life will be just like that of people who have plenty of things, but there is no hope of life eternal through wealth'. Maitreyi spurns the riches of the world remarking: 'What shall I do with that which will not make me immortal?' Yajnavalkya recognizes the spiritual fitness of his wife and teaches her the highest wisdom. This lesson, we should realize, is not to glorify poverty. Nor is it a piece of life-negating ascetism. Instead, the deeper meaning of this lesson is to see beyond all that is temporal and fleeting, and realize the power of the eternal/absolute *Self*. Because 'not for the sake of the worlds are the worlds dear, but the worlds are dear for the sake of the *Self*'. In fact, as Yajnavalkya replies, 'by the seeing of, by the hearing of, by the thinking of, by the understanding of the *Self*, everything is known' (BU II: 4.1-II: 4.5). A lesson of this kind, I assume, inspired all those who sought to enlighten us, and gave us the courage to stand up, and strive for a new civilization that the aggressive proponents of the market-oriented, media-induced, pleasure-seeking 'global' culture would never be able to imagine.

The art of resistance I am talking about is, therefore, not just an act of negation; it is essentially an affirmation of a new world. It is in this context that I wish to mention that culture should not be equated solely with its external forms and symbols. What is really important to realize is the basic ideal beneath these artefacts, and how culture is actually lived and experienced. Let us, therefore, strive for a global culture that rests on the ideals of harmony, reciprocity and aesthetic calmness. Once these ideals are clear we would be able to see beyond mere external forms and artefacts. For example, I would not feel guilty if, at times, I wear Levi's jeans, and eat a McDonald's hamburger, so long as I am not carried away by what these symbols otherwise seek to represent: a ruthlessly standardized consumptionist culture. Likewise, there is nothing great if I wear *khadi*, and listen to *bhajan* songs, but remain aggressive and consumptionist in everyday life. In fact, the taste of one's culture is the life one leads—its deeper meaning. That is why, the global culture we are striving for should overcome the burden of external forms, and internalize the ethos of harmony and reciprocity. In such a global culture Marx's humanism, Gandhi's prayer, the painting of Michelango, the aesthetic of temple architecture, the egalitarianism of liberal democracy, the passion of black poetry, and the experience of collective ecstasy in folk arts—all have their legitimate space so long as we experience calmness and reciprocity.

Yes, such a global culture has to be lived and experienced; it is not something that can be purchased in the shopping mall. Globalization is essentially about this unifying experience rather than a journey towards mechanical standardization when everyone is seduced to use the same brand, and the same product. Globalization is, therefore, not a technological spectacle, even though technologies help us to overcome geographical boundaries. Globalization, as I am trying to put forward, is about the elasticity of human mind and culture: the way we evolve, grow and embrace the larger world. It is a deep/intimate experience of oneness: the experience that leads one to understand the suffering of the next-door neighbour, the experience that inspires an African to read Dostoyvesky, and shed tears, and the experience that leads people in Australia to help the tsunami victims in Sri Lanka. It is not something that has to take place only in the cyber space (Wilson, 1997). It is about real concern and connectivity.

Let us strive for this new global culture, and resist the burden of excessive consumerism, technologization and depthlessness.

3

Transcending Limiting Identities: Striving for an Inclusive World

I have already reflected on modernity and globalization. And I have argued that it is desirable to evolve a spiritually regenerated modernity, and create a truly dialogic space to resist the ongoing process of asymmetrical globalization, and make it more humane and egalitarian. This is indeed a challenging task that requires a high degree of inner strength: the ability to cultivate one's mind, and grow open, inclusive and accommodative. In other words, we are striving for a culture that inspires us to long for the fusion of horizons. It is like striving for a culture in which one is not just a Tamil, a Dalit, an Englishman, a woman or a Muslim. Instead, one sees the limits to these segmented identities, and tries to broaden one's mind.

The social reality we confront, however, tells us a different story. We are driven by all sorts of limiting identities emanating from caste, ethnicity, language, religion, gender and nationality. These identities tend to determine our politics and worldviews. The world, as a result, becomes a site of identity conflict, ethnocentrism, racism, colonialism, casteism and parochialism. All these are symptoms of a culture that restricts and limits the human mind. Yes, it seems impossible to live without identities. Because there cannot be any abstract humanity. We all have our historical memories, local traditions, languages and cultural specificities. We are situated in time and space. And social identities are unlikely to escape us. What is, however, possible is to experience these identities as fluid and inclusive, and engage in a process of creative/dialogic assimilation. It is indeed possible not to be limited by segmented identities. In this chapter I wish to reflect on this complex dialectic—the formation and transcendence of identities.

It would not be wrong to say that what distinguishes man is his social identity. He lives in a shared/inter-subjective world with the other fellow members. He cannot imagine his existence—the language he speaks, the gestures he responds to, the symbols he emits, and the way he communicates—without taking into account the behaviour of others. His consciousness, thinking, feeling and acting are situated in the matrix of social relationships he is engaged in. It is in this sense that, if we borrow G.H. Mead's remarkable insight, man's 'self' arises in the process of social experience and activity (Mead, 1934: 135–226). Mead's analogy is indeed interesting. If I play a game, my action is determined by my assumption of the others who too are playing it. What I do, or the way I play is being controlled by my being everyone else on that team. Likewise, when I live in a community I need to take into account the attitude of what Mead would have regarded as 'the generalized other'. 'It is in the form of the generalized other that the social process influences the behavior of the individuals in it' (Ibid: 155). This is not to suggest that man is merely a puppet absolutely identical with his 'social self'—without any innovation and creativity. Mead does distinguish the 'I' from the 'me'. Yes, the 'me' is socially constructed; here is a conventional, habitual individual having those habits and responses which everyone had. Nevertheless, the 'I' gives a sense of freedom and initiative. It is something that is never entirely calculable; it brings the elements of novelty. What is sociologically significant is that everyday living in a community is impossible without the presence of those organized sets of attitudes that constructs 'me'. In a way,

Mead gives us an insight into the formation of social identities. Needless to add, the social groups man lives in—caste, ethnicity, gender and nationality—do shape these identities.

When I evolve a social identity—say, a caste/ethnic/religious identity—it defines me, gives me a sense of belonging, and a shared heritage. I like to believe that I have a distinctive language that I share with the other fellow members who too belong to the same community. Likewise, I have a caste, a religion and a nationality. This self-definition assures me, recognizes me, and gives me stability—a sense of continuity. Yes, I definitely have a language, a religion and a nationality. I cannot exist in a cultural void. But when I allow this self-definition to restrict and constrain me, I erect a wall, a boundary: 'we' vs. 'they', or our religion vs. their religion! These dualities, history suggests, tend to become oppressive and hierarchical. Is it then possible to have an altogether different orientation to social identities? Let us formulate these queries in a more concrete fashion. We often experience the overwhelming presence of a dominant identity. Depending on the specificity of the historic situation, it is possible to over-emphasize one's ethnic, caste, linguistic, religious or national identity as the dominant one. But then, is it really desirable or even possible for the dominant identity to envelop the complexity of one's entire being? Look at my own case. When I speak Bengali in my family, eat Bengali food, read Bengali poetry, and listen to Bengali music, I affirm my existence as a Bengali. When I watch, say, a *Bharatanatyam* programme, I transcend my 'Bengaliness', and experience myself as an 'Indian' taking part in our collective heritage. Or, when I come to the university, face my students who belong to different states and nations, I see myself as a 'teacher' having a more cosmopolitan/inclusive identity. Or, imagine myself reading William Blake:

My mother taught me underneath a tree
And sitting down before the heat of day,
She took me on her lap and kissed me,
And pointing to the east began to say.

Look on the rising sun: there God does live
And gives his light, and gives his heat away.
And flowers and trees and beasts and men receive
Comfort in morning joy in the noon day.

(Quoted in Bloom and Trilling, 1973:71)

Do I remain just a Bengali or an Indian? Or, do I become truly universal realizing what the poet regarded as our shared innocence? Herein lies the moot question: Who am I? Can I negotiate with all my social identities without allowing any of these to limit myself? Can I, therefore, grow broader and universal without losing the multiple colours of my being? Or, am I just a confused, schizophrenic and conflict-ridden being? Possibly I am a *dialogic being* striving for our shared humanity.

Let us also think of the implications of these identities in a multi-ethnic, multi-religious and multi-linguistic society like ours. Is unity possible when we see the proliferation of segmented identities, when, as K.S. Singh's mega project suggests, there are 4635 communities all over India, and 325 languages belonging to 12 different language families? (Singh, 2002) This is like asking a pertinent question: Is India truly a collective having a shared culture and heritage? Or, is India merely a construct: a centralized state executing the will of the dominant community, and imposing itself on diverse cultural identities? Likewise, what does happen to all these identities in a global society? Should we continue to hate one another? Or, is a new order emerging in which differences, far from confining us to isolated islands, create the very foundation of an alternative experience of unity: unity amidst differences through the perpetual process of dialogic conversation, assimilation and accommodation?

In other words, the questions we are raising in this chapter are the following:

1. How are identities constituted? And why do these identities continue to play an important role in shaping one's life and politics?
2. What are the limitations of these identities? Can we transcend these constraints?
3. What does it mean to strive for a culture in which differences emanating from multiple identities, far from posing obstacles, create a situation conducive to the process of assimilation and syncretism?

I
Complex Domain of Identities

Identities often appear to be 'natural'—something man is born with. But the fact is that identities are socially constructed through cultural practices and socialization. Take, for instance, what is often being regarded as innate/given, something rooted in biology itself—one's gender identity. Thanks to cultural anthropologists and sociologists, we now know that gender is not sex, and the process of growing up as 'masculine' or 'feminine' is essentially a cultural construct. Yes, one is born as a male or a female. But this biological facticity is transformed into an attitude, a belief, an ideal through family socialization, school curriculum and religious beliefs, and eventually one acquires a 'masculine' or a 'feminine' identity. In fact, I am tempted to refer to Leela Dube's brilliant work, the way 'by focusing on aspects of the process of socialization of Hindu girls through rituals and ceremonies, the use of language, and practices within and in relation to the family', she shows how women are produced as 'gendered subjects' (Dube, 2001:87–118). As girls grow up in patrilineal India they realize that male children are privileged, and they are repeatedly reminded of their temporary membership in the natal family. The rituals/ceremonies like *Durga puja* and *Gauri puja* convey a significant message that they are destined to be transferred from the natal home to that of the husband. For instance, in a Bengali wedding before leaving her natal home with the bridegroom, the bride stands with her back towards the house and throws a handful of rice over the shoulder. This, argues Dube, signifies that a woman has returned the rice that she had consumed until then and has absolved herself of the debt to the natal family. Not solely that. The 'purity' of the pre pubertal stage is reaffirmed by the custom of worshipping and the special ritual of feeding virgin girls on special occasions like *navaratri*. No wonder, the onset of puberty is a turning point. She is reminded that her time has finally come; she has grown big, and become a woman. In Karnataka, for instance, at her first menstruation, a girl is fed dry coconut, milk, ghee, certain fruits, a mixture of jaggery and sesame seeds. Moreover, it is customary for the relatives to bring gifts. The story goes on. Women grow up with blessings and *vratas* for getting a husband like *Shiva* and *Vishnu*. In fact, these practices constitute 'femininity'; a woman is led to internalize the 'feminine' ideal of a polite being with considerable degree of tolerance and self restraint:

> A girl should walk with soft steps—so soft that they are barely audible to others. Taking long strides denotes masculinity. Girls are often rebuked for jumping, running, rushing to a place, and hopping. These movements are considered indicative of masculine behaviour, unbecoming of a female...A girl has to be careful about her posture. She should not sit cross-legged or with her legs wide apart. Keeping one's knees close together while sitting, standing, or sleeping is 'decent' and indicates a sense of shame and modesty. 'Don't stand like a man' is a common rebuke to make a girl aware of the demands of femininity (Ibid: 105).

This is the way, Dube adds, a woman is made. She is not expected to be ambitious, aggressive and demanding. The quality of self-denial defines her. If a girl continues to cry and shout for food because she is hungry, she is teased about her lack of self-restraint. She must internalize the ideal of *Annapurna*: the unfailing supplier of food. 'This ideal, which has an aesthetic appeal and which sets out privation and sacrifice as defining characteristics of the feminine moral character generates a set of dispositions wherein a woman has to think of others before herself and ought not to care about what is being left for her' (Ibid: 111–12).

This is just an example that shows how identities are socially constructed. In fact, the identities that are often seen as 'given' or 'ascriptive' acquire their significance only through carefully evolved cultural practices. For instance, I may be born in a 'Brahmin' family; but whether or not I acquire a 'Brahmin' identity depends on the way I am socialized, and trained to separate myself from 'non-Brahmins'. In other words, it is important whether I see myself belonging to a subjectively self-conscious community that establishes rigid criteria for inclusion into and exclusion from the group. Likewise, the potency of one's ethnic identity depends on the intensity of the cultural practices. I often recall the way one grows up as a 'Bengali' in West Bengal. The specific festivals and ceremonies like *Durga puja*, Bengali New Year, and Tagore's birthday reinforce one's 'Bengali' identity. At school one is constantly reminded of the distinctiveness of Bengali language, its pride and history; one is told about its heroes and icons: Khudiram, Vivekananda and Netaji. One grows up with this self-perception that celebrates visible cultural markers; one knows that one is 'different' from, say, a 'Bihari', an 'Oriya' or a 'Madrasi'! As I look at my own days in Bengal, I realize how often my identity has been interrogated. Am I a 'true' Bengali or a Maithili Brahmin? The fact that I am 'Pathak', not Chatterjee or Banerjee has not been easily appreciated, particularly by those who wish to be certain about their distinctive identity, and its fixed boundaries and borders.

The point that I am trying to emphasize is that one is not born with an identity. Identities are socially constructed. And this seems to be the reason why identities, no matter how 'natural' they look, can also be transcended. As a matter of fact, radical politics like feminism and Marxism often perceives alternative cultural practices through which one transcends socially imposed, particularly stigmatized identities, and seeks to become more universal and humane. Furthermore, as Mead himself suggested, both aspects of the 'I' and 'me' are essential to the self in its full expression. That is why, even when the 'me' is habitual and conventional or a conformist, we come across innovative situations when the assertion of the creative 'I' becomes inevitable, when we see a person 'who replies to the organized attitude in a way that makes a significant difference' (Mead, 1934: 200). In other words, man is not merely an actor reading the script which has already been written for him; he can alter it. And that is where, I believe, lies man's hope.

It is in this context that I feel tempted to share with the readers an inspiring Gandhian experiment: the assertion of the 'I' aspect of his personality, his ability to overcome his 'caste identity'. Mohandas—a young man of Rajkot—was willing to go to England for higher studies. His caste people, however, disliked the idea, because it was thought that 'religion forbids voyages abroad'. They apprehended that it would mean bad and unethical practices. Yet, Mohandas acquired the courage to disobey the verdict of the caste association, and become an 'outcaste' (Gandhi, 1927:29–30). He reinterpreted life in an altogether different mode. He felt that he had promised his mother that he would not touch 'wine, women and meat', and nothing was more important than his mother's blessing and permission. The story he narrated was immensely revealing:

> Meanwhile my caste-people were agitated over my going abroad...If I dared to do so, I ought to be brought to book! A general meeting of the caste was called and I was summoned to appear before it. I went. How I suddenly managed to muster up courage I do not know. Nothing daunted, and without the slightest hesitation, I came before the meeting. The Sheth—the headman of the community—who was distantly related to me and had been on very good terms with my father, thus accosted me:
>
> 'In the opinion of the caste, your proposal to go to England is not proper. Our religion forbids voyages abroad. We have also heard that it is not possible to live there without compromising our religion. One is obliged to eat and drink with Europeans'.
>
> To which I replied: 'I do not think it is at all against our religion to go to England. I intend going there for further studies. And I have already solemnly promised to my mother to abstain from three things you fear most. I am sure the vow will keep me safe' (Ibid:29).

These experiments—or these humble, yet dissenting voices—I assume, transformed Mohandas into the Mahatma. And we too begin to realize that identities, far from being fixed, are negotiable; it is not altogether impossible to alter one's prescribed identity!

Not all identities are, however, of the same kind. Some are broader, and some terribly limited in their scope. Take, for instance, caste as one's identity. When one sees oneself as a Brahmin, one is certainly distinguishing oneself from non-Brahmins. Or, when one asserts one's Dalit identity one is conveying a message that one is not united with, say, the hierarchical 'Hindu' fold; one is oppressed and marginalized. In other words, when caste becomes one's primary identity one does not expand much; one's universe remains limited by rigid caste boundaries. But then, if we contrast caste with, say, class we get an altogether different picture. Yes, class in the classical Marxian sense is broader in its scope and horizon. A class that becomes conscious of itself, and its historic mission, it would be argued by the adherents of classical Marxism, succeeds in overcoming primordial/segmented/limiting identities. Because the commonality of economic/material interests—or the Marxism assertion that 'I am what I produce, and the way I produce'—would be the unifying ground. I may be a male/Brahmin and Bengali. Yet, in the Marxian sense it is not difficult for me to have a close affinity and work as a comrade with a Tamil/Dalit female worker, if both of us see ourselves belonging to the proletariat or the working class. In a way, classical Marxism is immensely optimistic about the potency of class interests. No wonder, as the *Manifesto* declared, the communists, even when fighting their battle in the national domain, are capable of having an international outlook. In the Marxian scheme of class struggle and social transformation, ethnic/caste identities become somewhat secondary. This seems to be the reason why we have often witnessed a tension-ridden relationship between the Marxists on the one hand, and the proponents of caste politics on the other. Likewise, it can also be said that 'nationality' or, say, one's 'Indian' identity is much broader than one's caste, ethnic or regional identity. As 'Indians' we are repeatedly reminded of our collective heritage: our shared memories, the continual process of cultural assimilation, and the blurring of ethnic/regional differentiation.

What is, however, important to note is the complex interplay of these broader and smaller identities. In fact, in the politico-cultural realm we often notice the demystification of the so-called broader/universal identities. Instead, we see the assertion of differences relating to the multiplicity of caste/ethnic identities; we become aware of the internal cleavage/conflict. Take, for instance, the 'national' urge to consolidate our 'Indian' identity. I wish to give a specific illustration from the freedom struggle. Yes, this historic struggle for decolonization was a turning-point, and a great event in our collective life. It gave us a mission to unite and work together. This unitary feeling was reflected in the formation of the Indian National Congress, pan-Indian mass movements, widespread mobilization, and above all, the influence of charismatic leaders like Gandhi, Tagore and Nehru who could transcend their limiting identities and derive their legitimacy from their universal appeal. But then, if we look at history, we notice that this immensely emotive shared Indianness was also problematized; the depressed castes and classes, for instance, interrogated it, and deconstructed the nation by revealing its internal cleavage. As I would argue, a classic illustration of this complex interplay of nation and caste could be seen in the political assertion of B.R. Ambedkar, his critical engagement with Gandhi and the Indian National Congress. Even when nationalism was at its peak, Ambedkar did not hesitate to argue that the primary enemy, far from being imperialism, was the tyranny of casteism:

> The Depressed classes, surrounded by enemies on all sides, could not afford to fight on all fronts at once. I, therefore, decided to fight the two thousand year old tyranny and oppression of the caste Hindus and secure social equality of the Depressed classes before anything else (Quoted in Omvedt, 1994: 212).

It was, therefore, not surprising that Ambedkar did not feel comfortable with Gandhi—the way he represented India. Gandhi, for him, was the 'dictator of India' who took us to the 'dark age'. This conflict, we know, manifested itself rather sharply in the issue of the separate electorates for the Dalits. Gandhi opposed it, because he feared that it would lead to 'political division'. Ambedkar disagreed; he felt that there was no reason to pretend that we were united.

He questioned Gandhi, and his right to represent the whole India, including the interests of the depressed classes:

> The Mahatma has always been claiming that the Congress stands for the Depressed classes and that the Congress represented the Depressed classes more than I or my colleagues can do. To that claim I can only say that it is one of the many false claims which irresponsible people keep on making, although the persons connected with regard to these claims have invariably been denying them...The Depressed classes are not in the Congress (Ibid: 170–71).

Gandhi, we know, insisted on the need for restoring the national unity. Eventually some kind of a solution emerged in the form of the Poona Pact. But never did Ambedkar feel shy of expressing his anguish over Gandhi's 'moral blackmail'!

As a matter of fact, this bold assertion of differences and the resultant demystification of a unitary identity of 'Indianness' characterize our times. Instead of a broader civilizational identity, we witness the resistance emanating from those who proclaim their differences, their anguish, and their right to their alternative and autonomous identities. It is in this context that I wish to speak of a book that seems to have aroused the imagination of contemporary social scientists in India. In fact, as I engage myself with Kancha Ilaiah's work, I realize the intensity of the discontent: the way someone belonging to a marginalized/ oppressed caste expresses his anguish, demystifies the so-called 'Hindu' identity, and asserts his reason for not being a Hindu (Ilaiah, 1996). In his text filled with autobiographical experiences, powerful rhetoric and passionate sociology, Ilaiah intends to convey a strong message: Hinduism (and he equates it with Brahminism) cannot be the religion of Dalitbahujans; their identity is radically different from Hindu identity. He recalls his own childhood, the process of growing up as someone belonging to the *Kurumma* caste in an unknown Andhra Pradesh village. There was nothing that could unite him with the Brahmins/Baniyas and other upper caste Hindus. Ilaiah comes with a hammer, and contrasts these two cultures. The Brahmins/Baniyas live in a different world. They oppress and dominate. Their sexual life, says Ilaiah, is hypocritical; their religion is fascist; their family life is authoritarian. They are ritualistic and non-productive. They hate labour, and entertain useless leisure. Their culture is imposed on the rest of society. Education becomes hegemonic; seldom does it give legitimacy to the alternative culture of the Dalitbahujans:

> As we were growing up, stepping into higher classes, the textbooks taught us stories which we had never heard in our families. The stories of Rama and Krishna, poems from the Puranas, the names of two epics called *Ramayana* and *Mahabharata* occurred repeatedly...I distinctly remember how alien all these names appeared to me. Many of the names were not known in my village. The name of Kalidasa was as alien to us as the name of Shakespeare (Ibid: 13).

Ilaiah's anger is unbounded. He does not spare even the Marxists. He alleges that the communist upper castes did not give up the Hindu way of life. Their friendship, their marriage relations remained confined to their own caste circles. For Ilaiah, never did these Brahmin communists critique Hindu Gods. His manifesto, however, seeks to resist this trend; it pleads for an alternative identity for the Dalitbahujans. Yes, this requires immense faith and confidence in their own culture which, he argues, is more productive and life-affirming than Brahminism. He, therefore, contrasts Hindu ideals from their ideals, and inspires his audience. For example, Hindu gods and goddesses are institutionalized in a most brazen anti-

Dalitbahujan fashion. *Indra,* he argues, led the mass extermination of the Indus Valley-based Adi-Dravidians, who were also Adi-Dalitbahujans; *Brahma*-the god of wisdom-is armed with the weapons to attack the Dalitbahujans; *Vishnu's chakram* is designed to kill all those who rebel against the Brahmins, and an epic like the *Ramayana* is an account of the aggression aimed at Brahminizing the Dalitbahujan society of South India turning it into a Brahminizing patriarchy! But, argues Ilaiah, the gods and goddesses they worship are truly democratic, egalitarian and humane. Take, for instance, *Pochamma*—the most popular Dalitbahujan goddess in Andhra Pradesh:

> Unlike Sita, her gender role is not specified. Nobody knows about Pochamma's husband. Nobody considers her inferior or useless because she does not have a husband. The contrast between Saraswathi and Lakshmi, on the one hand, and Pochamma on the other is striking. Pochamma is independent. She does not pretend to serve any man. Her relationship to human beings is gender-neutral, caste-neutral and class-neutral. She is supposed to take care of everyone in the village. She herself relates to nature, production and procreation...She understands all languages and all dialects. The people can speak with her in their own tongues; a Brahmin can go and talk to her in Sanskrit; an English person can go and talk to her in English (Ibid: 92).

Likewise, unlike 'brahminical authoritarianism', their culture is open, democratic, organic, and more close to nature. It values labour and productive skill. It does not entertain *mantra, puja* and *tapasya.* It is scientific. No wonder, it redefines knowledge and courage:

> In our real life a knowledgeable person is one who has knowledge of social functions—one who knows about

> sheep-breeding, agriculture, rope making; one who can diagnose the nature of the diseases of animals and human beings. A courageous person is one who can fight tigers, lions, snakes, wild bulls; who can travel deep into forests, swim the rivers and find the missing goats and sheep (Ibid: 17).

Ilaiah, as I have said, asserts the Dalitbahujan identity, and its sharp difference from the dominant Hindu identity. For him, the goal is clear. His manifesto ends with a note that seems to be in tune with the politics of differences:

> If the Brahminwaada represents the ideal for them, the Dalitwaada should be the ideal for us. Just as they are shouting from their rooftops (and they have very big houses) 'Hinduize India', we must shout from our toddy palms, from the fields, from treetops, and from Dalibahujanwaadas, 'Dalitize India'. We must shout 'we hate Hinduism, we hate Brahminism, we love our culture and more than anything, we love ourselves' (Ibid: 132).

Even though he simplifies Hinduism and romanticizes/ essentializes his own culture, one thing is certain. His anguish is real, and it is likely to fragment our society further, and intensify the conflict-ridden identity politics, unless some innovative changes are made in our society.

The recognition of differences, as I am arguing, has acquired tremendous legitimacy in contemporary social science. As a result, the hegemony of a grand or totalizing identity is suspected, and the co-existence of multiple collectivities having distinctive identities is seen as a virtue of pluralism. Not surprisingly, the idea of a grand 'Indian' identity is often problematized. In fact, this critique of a stable/cohesive Indian identity (or Indian nationality) has come not just from the oppressed castes; it has also come from diverse collectivities characterized by their distinctive cultural/linguistic identities. It is feared that the very idea of India as a nation would go against the ethos of pluralism. In recent times, T.K. Oommen has been asserting this thesis quite boldly (Oommen, 1997: 2004). He is categorical that India is not, and cannot be a nation. Instead, it is a configuration of many nations co-existing under one polity. Yet, as Oommen seeks to warn us, we often tend to forget this basic truth, and begin to project India as a nation. And it has devastating consequences. It creates a hierarchical socio-political milieu in which the dominant community hijacks the agenda of the 'nation', suppresses the cultural/linguistic aspirations of the rest of society, and treats them as 'parochial' and 'anti-national'. India as a nation is an idea that Oommen loathes, and in his characteristic argumentative style he makes his point. He refutes the arguments of those who plead for India as a nation. For instance, it has often been argued that India is a nation because of its civilizational unity. This kind of thesis, argues Oommen, invariably refers to the Hindu culture as the element which provides the essential unity. But he sees a danger; it negates the contributions of the Muslims and the British. Again, there are some who are more vocal, and regard Hinduism as the basis of the Indian nation. It homogenizes Hinduism; it refuses to see the internal hierarchy, and the resultant discontent within Hinduism itself. Furthermore, 'in such a conceptualization of nation one of the religious collectivities gets rehabilitated at the centre of the hegemonic collectivity, relegating others to the periphery and marginalizing them' (Oommen, 2004: 29). He sees the manifestations of this hegemony in diverse socio-political spheres. First, the 'constitutional expansionism', he argues, denies the identity of minority religions of Indian origin. A striking example is, of course, the Hindu Code Bill—the way it incorporates the Jains, the Buddhists and the Sikhs, and treats all of them as 'Hindus'. Second, Islam and Christianity are often perceived as 'products of conquest and colonization'. Third, only the deprived sections among the Hindus, the Buddhists and the Sikhs get the benefits of protective discrimination. This, according to Oommen, is certainly unfair to Islam and Christianity.

Oommen is also not happy with those who appear to be more refined and sophisticated, and plead for a 'composite culture' as the basis of the Indian nation. While this composite culture thesis emphasizes the fusion of Hinduism and Islam, it tends to ignore the pre and non-Aryan peoples—the Dravidians, SCs and STs. Oommen goes further, and challenges the philosophy of compositeness itself, because 'compositeness implies assimilation and fusion, and hence is the very antithesis of pluralism, which is the celebration of diversity in order to facilitate the co-existence of cultures, in spite of their distinctiveness' (Ibid: 26). Again, there are some who are willing to recognize the existence of 'little nations or 'sub-nations', but under the umbrella of the great Indian nation. It is an ambiguous position. While it accepts the reality of distinctive cultural collectivities, it does not deny the centrality of the Indian nation. Because it fears that 'if these little nationalities are recognized as nations they would necessarily clamour for their exclusive sovereign states' (Ibid: 37).

As Oommen would argue, there is no reason to insist that India is a nation. Instead, it is high time we accepted India as a 'multinational state'. India, for him, is essentially a politico-legal entity that consists of multiple nations. For example, you are a Tamil; Tamil is your nationality. And I am a Bengali; Bengali is my nationality. Nationality is a solid cultural experience, because 'nation is a tangible entity defined in terms of concrete objective characteristics such as a common homeland and a language'. You as a Tamil may feel more affinity with a Tamil from Sri Lanka, and I with a Bengali from Bangladesh. There is, however, nothing intensely shared cultural experience (say, a common language) that can make two of us belong to the same nation. India is, therefore, not our nation. It is only a geographical territory—a politico-legal entity. It is the Indian state that gives us *citizenship*. As citizens (not as people having same nationality) we live in India, and the state is expected to treat us as equal citizens. Citizenship and nationality, Oommen argues repeatedly, should not be equated. In fact, 'unlinking nationality and citizenship is an imperative if the society is to be rendered open'.

Oommen's message is clear. There is no broader identity called shared Indianness. We are destined to live with our specific nationalities (as Tamils, Bengalis, etc.). This is what pluralism is all about. Any attempt to impose an over-arching Indian identity would disturb this plurality. India cannot give us a cultural identity; it can give us only citizenship! While Oommen's celebration of pluralism is praiseworthy, his thesis, however, suffers from two shortcomings. First, he reduces India into a mere politico-legal state; he deprives it of its emotive cultural appeal. What he forgets is that even though our languages and dietary practices are different, India is in our collective consciousness. India, in fact, is a perpetual process of becoming. Yes, Buddha, Sankara and Kabir enter our collective consciousness. Subbalaxmi and Lata Mangeshkar transcend all regional barriers, and *masala dosa*, *samosa*, cricket and Bollywood acquire a pan-Indian character. It is indeed absurd to say that we have nothing that unites us except the election ID and the ration card! Second, he refuses to acknowledge that there is also a constant urge to broaden one's horizon and universe. I may be a Bengali, but it is also my urge to broaden my horizon through a dialogic conversation with a Tamil or a Sikh or a European. In other words, unlike what Oommen thinks, my identity is not something fixed—defined once for all; it is perpetually evolving, and experimenting with itself. I am a Bengali. My wife is a Maithili. And my daughter may grow up as more than a mere Bengali or a Maithili—an Indian, or even more than that, possibly a universal being! In other words, our life—even the lives of ordinary mortals like us—teaches us that there is also an equally important urge to strive for something broader, more inclusive and universal. Oommen's thesis does not seem to have this scope. In the name of pluralism it ends up legitimizing one's limited/restricted identity. It forgets that authentic pluralism is not just about one's right to retain one's cultural difference; it is also about one's ability to celebrate a sense of humility, and to learn from others, and become more than just oneself. Yes, contemporary social science speaks of multiple identities and resultant differences. It is indeed a turn towards political democratization. But then, there is something far deeper—democratization of the human mind. Here social science fails, and the wisdom of the poets, saints, mystics and revolutionaries inspires. I have often wondered how Oommen would characterize people like Kabir, Gandhi and Tagore. Were they confined only to their distinctive cultural collectivities—Kabir amongst the weavers in Benares, Gandhi amongst the Gujarati baniyas, and Tagore amongst the educated Bengali *bhadralok*? Or, were they perpetually transcending their 'nationalities' and limited identities, and becoming truly universal? These are complex issues relating to identity transcendence: overcoming little identities, and striving for something more universal and inclusive.

II
Hierarchy and Conflict

But before everything else, we need to ask yet another important sociological question: Why is it that identities assert themselves, and contest the grand order? A major reason, I guess, is that identities, far from existing as symmetrical differences, are often graded, ranked and hierarchized. This dualism (or asymmetrical power relations) causes severe pain and anguish. And possibly as the ethos of democratization enters the larger socio-political life, the hitherto marginalized groups having 'inferior' identities, or 'low' ranking begin to protest, and contest the entire ideology that legitimizes these hierarchies. Had there been symmetry and equality one would not have become possibly obsessed with one's identity. Instead, we could have seen a social milieu conducive to dialogic conversation. But then, in a social environment characterized by hierarchy, unevenness and asymmetry, limiting identities, far from withering away, become terribly conscious of themselves. Identities begin to matter—for privilege, exploitation, domination and marginalization.

As a result, we witness the assertion of what social scientists regard as 'identity politics'. Before we know more about it, it would be worthwhile to reflect on the very principle of hierarchy, particularly in the context of our own society which seems to be the chief reason for confining ourselves to our little identities. A striking illustration is, of course, the hierarchy of *varnas* (or castes). What strikes the imagination of indologists and sociologists alike is, of course, the much-talked about *Manusmriti*—the scripture that sanctifies this hierarchy. A careful reader of the laws of Manu would find an elaborated principle of hierarchy in the classification of the four *varnas*, their origin, their assigned duties and responsibilities, and their status in the order of things. We are told that in order to protect the universe, 'Brahma, the most resplendent one, assigned separate duties and occupations to those who sprang from his mouth (Brahmanas), arms (Kshatriyas), thighs (Vaisyas), and feet (Sudras) (I: 87). It was said that 'to Brahmanas, He assigned teaching and studying (the Veda), sacrificing for their own benefit and for others, giving and accepting (of alms)' (I: 88). Likewise, the Kshatriyas were commanded 'to protect the people, to bestow gifts, to offer sacrifices, and to study (the Veda) (I: 89). And the Vaisyas were required 'to tend cattle, to bestow gifts, to offer sacrifices, to study (the Veda), to trade, to lend money and to cultivate land' (I: 90). But things were quite different for the Sudras. 'One occupation only the lord prescribed to the Sudra, to serve meekly even these (other) three castes' (I: 91). This division of labour, it doesn't take much time to understand, implies not just differences, but a strict principle of grading, ranking and hierarchy. That is why, 'a Brahmana, be he ignorant or learned, is a great divinity, just as the fire, whether carried forth (for the performance of a burnt-oblation) or not carried forth, is a great divinity' (IX: 317). And even the kings were commanded 'to worship Brahmanas who are well versed in the threefold sacred science and learned (in polity), and follow their advice' (VII: 37). Because 'when the Kshatriyas become in any way overbearing towards the Brahmanas, the Brahmanas themselves shall duly restrain them; for the Kshatriyas sprang from the Brahmanas' (IX: 20). Likewise, 'a Vaisya must never conceive this wish, I will not keep cattle' (IX: 328). No wonder, 'as the Brahmana sprang from (Brahman's) mouth, as he was the first-born, and as he possesses the Veda, he is by right the lord of this whole creation' (I: 93). This hierarchy could also be seen in the principle of exclusion: the way the 'twice-born' castes were repeatedly reminded of the pollution emanating from the 'impurity' of the Sudras. No wonder, 'twice-born men who, in their folly, wed wives of the low (Sudra) caste, soon degrade their children to the state of Sudras' (III: 15). Not solely that. The Brahmanas were commanded 'not to dwell in a country where the rulers are Sudras' (IV: 61); they were not supposed to 'give advise to a Sudra' (IV: 80), and they must avoid reciting the Vedas 'in the presence of Sudras' (IV: 49). This grading, ranking and hierarchy could be seen in its extreme form when we were told that 'a once-born man (a Sudra), who insults a twice-born man with grass invective, shall have his tongue cut out' (VIII: 270). Or, 'with whatever limb a man of a low caste does hurt to (a man of the three) higher (castes), even that limb shall be cut off' (VIII: 279).

In our times one book that seems to have aroused tremendous interest in this elaborated principle of hierarchy is Louis Dumont's *Homo Hierarchicus* (Dumont, 1970). Although Dumont was a French scholar, he looked at this principle of hierarchy with great care and precision. Yes, he contrasted Indian society from the individual-centric, egalitarian Western society. What was, however, significant was that never did he feel shy of expressing the limits to 'moral and political egalitarianism' of the West, and the need to learn from the principle of hierarchy:

> Man does not only think, he acts. He has not only ideas, but values. To adopt a value is to introduce hierarchy, and a certain consensus of values, a certain hierarchy of ideas, things and people, is indispensable to social life...Moreover, it is understandable and natural that hierarchy should encompass social agents and social categories. In relation to these more or less necessary requirements of social life, the ideal of equality, even if it is thought superior, is artificial...It represents a deliberate denial of a universal phenomenon in a restricted domain. We have no intention...of throwing doubt on this ideal. But it is well to understand to what extent it runs contrary to the general tendencies of societies, and hence how far our society is exceptional, and how difficult it is to realize this ideal (Ibid: 20).

Hierarchy, for Dumont, is not just ranking and grading. Hierarchy is the principle 'by which the elements of a whole are ranked in relation to the whole' (Ibid: 66). It is, therefore, important to note that 'the whole is founded on the necessary and hierarchical coexistence of the two opposites' (Ibid: 43). For example, as Dumont would interpret, the 'impurity' of the untouchable is conceptually inseparable from the 'purity' of the Brahman. The execution of impure tasks by some is necessary to the maintenance of purity of others. The two poles are equally necessary, though unequal. It was in this context that he looked at the scriptures, and saw the hierarchy of *varnas*, its complexity and subtlety:

> The hierarchy of varnas can be seen not as a linear order, but as a series of successive dichotomies or inclusions. The set of the four varnas divide the two: the last category that of the Sudra, is opposed to the block of the first three, whose members are 'twice-born' in the sense that they participate in initiation, second birth, and in the religious life in general. These twice-born in turn divide into two: the Vaishyas are opposed to the block formed by the Kshatriyas and the Brahmans, which in turn divides into two (Ibid: 67).

The hierarchy of *varnas*, for Dumont, helps us to understand the hierarchy of castes, because 'the *varnas* have the advantage of providing a model which is...universal throughout India' (Ibid: 73). As a matter of fact, this hierarchical principle is not limited only to caste identities; other identities too are hierarchized. For example, in a patriarchal society the differences between men and women no longer remain simple/symmetrical differences. As they grow up, and develop 'masculine' and 'feminine' identities, they are already hierarchized. Men are privileged, and women are subdued. A woman is seen to be an 'incomplete/castrated' man—with weak superego and conscience. No wonder, we see the anguish of Simone de Beauvoir when she writes: 'She is the incidental, the inessential. He is the subject; he is the Absolute—she is the 'Other'! (Beauvoir, 1986: 13). Women continue to bear the burden of this 'otherness'. Their humiliation, marginalization, and isolation from the 'active/rational/public domain' reduce them into silent role-performers; they bear only the 'legacy' of the male-directed culture they live in! Likewise, in a multi-ethnic society like ours not all ethnic identities are equally privileged. It is possible to see a distinctive hierarchy: the way some ethnic groups are seen as 'problematic', or 'backward', and kept under perpetual surveillance (not just through police and army, but through schools and religious institutions) in order to integrate them to the civilizational ethos of the 'mainstream'. Yes, we experience this ranking, grading and hierarchy of identities: 'forward' castes vs. 'backward' castes, men vs. women, and 'great' traditions vs. 'little' traditions. There is no way we can deny that it does not exist. But then, as I wish to argue, it is not, and should not be the end of history. It is possible—and I would say desirable—to have symmetrical differences, and also a politico-cultural practice that inspires us to see beyond these differences, and realize the deeper unity. This unity need not be uniformity; nor is it yet another name of hegemony. Instead, this unity, let us hope, makes differences comfortable, and yes open, humble and dialogic. Differences prevail, yet merge into the ocean of unity. Even if it appears to be difficult, it is a project worth-striving for. Because widening one's horizon ought to be seen as the virtue of the civilizing process.

III
Dialectic of Identity Politics

Before we reflect on this possibility or this desirable project, it is, however, important to know about the actual state of identity politics in India. As I have already indicated, a major reason behind the proliferation of identity politics in our times is that the hitherto subdued groups are overcoming the age-old silence, and refusing to be defined through the categories of the dominant group. No wonder, we see the growing challenge to some of the dominant ideologies of hierarchy: be it Brahminism or patriarchy or Hindu nationalism. Yes, India is being characterized by the intensity of identity politics. We are witnessing a struggle for recognition, for cultural autonomy and difference, for a legitimate space in the politico-economic arena. A careful student of India's political history knows how the centralizing ideology of, say, 'Hindi-Hindu nationalism' has been contested time and again by diverse ethnic groups. We need some illustrations to understand the gravity of the situation.

Let me recall how a self-conscious, proud, assertive Tamil identity once resisted the hegemony of Hindi, and aroused our imagination that linguistic pluralism could by no means be sacrificed in the name of some 'official/ national' language. We know that here is a strongly independent Dravidian linguistic identity. Furthermore, here is a land known for its prolonged history of resistance: the non-Brahman movement that distinguished the original Dravidian inhabitants from the Aryan intruders. We also know of E.V. Ramaswami Periyar: the way his 'self-respect' agenda gave a new momentum to the struggle for a distinctive Tamil identity. It was, therefore, not surprising that the Tamils could not tolerate a strange decision that the government of India took in 1965. It was decided that Hindi would replace English as an official language. The DMK organized massive protest; five Tamil students burned themselves to death, and in two weeks police firing had killed sixty people. It was indeed a reminder.

Likewise, the Punjab violence in the 1980s manifested yet another hidden tension: the tension that emerged out of a complex relationship between Hinduism and Sikhism. True, Sikhism, unlike Islam, is not seen as an 'alien' religion; its Indian origin, and its syncretism make it more intimate, almost a religion like 'ours'. Yet, it should not be forgotten that the Sikhs continue to demand an acknowledgement that they are a separate people to determine their own future and their relations with other peoples. How can we forget that there has been a consistent demand for an autonomous Sikh identity? True, in the1960s Saint Fateh Singh insisted that the Sikh 'political demand for a Punjabi Suba was not a religious communal demand for a Sikh majority state, but simply a linguistic demand. But then, Master Tara Singh—the other leading proponent of Sikh identity—had always been associated with the idea that the Sikhs were entitled to determine their own future in 1947, but had been deprived of it by the Congress. He also never hesitated to declare that the Punjabi Suba he envisioned was to be a Sikh-majority province. But then, the Indian government with its divide and rule policy, as Paul Brass argued (Brass, 1991:169–213), played its Machiavellian game, and paradoxically, it led to the *Bhindranwale* phenomenon: the demand for a separate/sovereign Khalistan, the all-pervasive violence, the Operation Bluestar, and eventually the assassination of Mrs. Indira Gandhi. Well, it is possible to argue that the Sikhs are not really discriminated against in India. After all, Sikh farmers are the most prosperous in the country; Sikh entrepreneurs have made their presence felt throughout India, and Sikhs are still heavily represented in the Indian armed forces. Yet, as Brass reminds us:

> Sikh perceptions of discrimination are not without foundation. It continues to rankle that the Punjabi Suba was the last linguistic state to be conceded in India, and only after two decades of agitation; that Punjabi-speaking Hindus lied about their mother tongue to prevent it; and that the provincial capital, Chandigarh, has till now still not been formally handed over to Punjab...The Akali political position is that, as a sovereign people, the Sikhs chose to join with India in 1947 in the belief that their separate political status would be recognized, but that they were instead betrayed, tricked, and manipulated so that they have had constantly to fight even to have their separate identity acknowledged (Ibid:200–01).

Similarly, the perpetually disturbed North East reminds us

of the politics of identity. Of the seven states located in the region, all—except Manipur and Tripura—were previously parts of Assam. The policy of Assam government in 1962 making Assamesse the official language led to an agitation for creating separate states in the area to protect the interests of the tribal. True, it resulted in the creation of seven states in the region. Yet, the problem remains: the refusal of the North East communities to accept their subsumption within Indian national identity. It should not be forgotten that the people of Mizo hill demanded separation not only from Assam but also from India. And the Nagas of Naga Hill district under the leadership of Phizo had wanted a separate independent state for the Nagas, and boycotted the 1952 election. Even though the government of India plays its 'divide and rule' game, there is no escape from the discontent and alienation resulting in militarization, insurgency and mutual suspicion. The reason is that, as some commentators have argued, the 'statist-nationalist' approach denies any place for local, regional and ethnic aspirations to articulate a position of power through its claims of identity (Biswas and Bhattacharjee, 2001).

No discussion on identity politics would be complete without looking at the tremendous vitality of caste politics in India. Yes, one's caste identity is a significant factor in Indian politics; liberal democracy, far from extinguishing caste consciousness, has given a new meaning to caste-based identity politics. A major reason is that the lower castes no longer accept their position in the social hierarchy. They refuse to accept that their lower economic status and the lack of respect from members of the higher castes are a 'given' in their social existence. Instead, as Myron Weiner argues, 'the widespread rejection of the ideological foundations of India's hierarchical social order gave them the confidence to mobilize and assert themselves' (Weiner, 2001). We know the history of the non-Brahman movement in the southern part of the country. We also know that by the 1950s there was a significant shift in power. In Tamil Nadu, for example, the Brahmin leadership was replaced by Nadras and other lower castes; in Andhra by Reddis and Kammas. Even in the northern part things began to change. True, for quite some time, the Congress used to get support of the Scheduled Castes and the Muslims. However, it failed to attract the middle castes. Ram Manohar Lohia tried to mobilize the backward castes, and Charan Singh—a Jat—brought a large section of the middle and backward castes into his party. And eventually we saw non-Brahmin, non-upper caste elites taking power, first the Jats, then the Yadavs, and by the latter part of the 1990s, UP had a Dalit Chief Minister. We also saw the historic implementation of the Mandal Commission recommendation for job reservation for the OBCs which drastically altered the political landscape in terms of the assertion of caste as one's socio-political identity.

> Paradoxically, as caste has become somewhat less important in determining individual life-chances, caste has become more salient as a political identity, and as an institutionalized element of civil society. There are now caste-based political parties, caste-based educational institutions and hostels, and caste-based housing societies...The tendency in India is toward institutional structures based upon caste that are not open and inclusive and which therefore nurture distrust and conflict between castes (Ibid: 220).

In this entire scenario of caste-based identity politics, the Dalit assertion is immensely significant. Because in this assertion of the hitherto subdued groups we see a language of resistance against Brahminism, and its implicit principle of hierarchy. We also see a new confidence, a heightened self-awareness of being a Dalit, and its distinctive symbols, literature and cultural expression. Yes, the historic *Mahad Satyagraha* in 1927 in which Ambedkar burnt a copy of the

Manusmriti was indeed a turning point. This confidence could be seen in the way. the Dalits critiqued what they regarded as Gandhi's 'paternalistic' attitude. Instead, they now began to look at themselves, their innate possibilities, and challenged the dominant Brahminic Hinduism and its principle of hierarchy. It was a struggle for recognition, a struggle for the abolishment of stigmatization and of all discriminations derived therefrom or connected with it. From the Dalit Panther movement in the 1970s to the political ascendancy of Mayawati and her Bahujan Samaj Party—we see this assertive identity politics. It has its own icons, own sybmols, own expressive idioms and language. Ambedkar, not Gandhi, is seen as a saviour; Dalit literature is distinguished from forward caste literature, and an 'emancipatory' religion like Buddhism is seen as an alternative to 'oppressive' Brahminical Hinduism. Possibly it is in this milieu of heightened identity politics that Kancha Ilaiah—with his characteristic polemical style—celebrates 'buffalo nationalism', and debunks the Hindu/Brahminic obsession with the 'purity' of the white cow (Ilaiah, 2004). The buffalo, for him, represents the whole Dravidian/Dalit Bahujan culture. It symbolizes that 'black is beautiful'; it means the 'end of racism'. Ilaiah's battle reflects the hunger for new symbols which the Dalits need to distinguish themselves:

> The buffalo is portrayed in Hindu iconography as the bearer of the God of Death, and as the demon killed by the Goddess Durga at the behest of Rama. It is unnecessary to point out the coercive message that these images send out to the people who love, rely on, care for, cultivate with, profit from, and prize the buffalo, and who have accomplished the feat of domesticating this unique animal. If there is one symbol that exalts the culture of the Dalit Bahujans and simultaneously brings the sophistry of Hindutva crashing down like a house of cards, it is the buffalo. Once we recognize this,

> we must work to construct a new, inclusive and just nationalism around the buffalo and all it stands for (Ibid: XXXI).

The assertion of women is yet another reflection of identity politics. True, social reform projects led by Raja Rammohun Roy and Ishwar Chandra Vidyasagar, and Gandhi's creative engagement with the freedom struggle were significant events that made us sensitive to the women's issue. But in recent times, 'new' women's movements that started emerging in the 1970s gave an altogether different dimension to the women's question. The movements led by divergent feminist groups and associations interrogated the prevalent patriarchal practices relating to sexual harassment, female infanticide, domestic violence and dowry death. Not solely that. The need for a feminist voice was felt, and some of the cherished beliefs regarding the status/identity of a woman were challenged. Possibly this assertion led to the proliferation of women's writings and feminist scholarship in contemporary India. The result is the heightened awareness of being a woman, and the need to re-examine nation, family, sexuality, culture and politics (Sangari and Vaid, 1989; Hasan, 1994). An outcome of this assertion, as we are seeing in recent times, is the growing pressure on the government to introduce a bill in Parliament regarding the reservation for women in legislative bodies. It would not be wrong to say that the principle of hierarchy is questioned, and women are persuaded to see themselves as the makers of their own world.

As a matter of fact, India seems to be a remarkably innovative site for identity politics. It is all around: ethnic groups striving for autonomy (Tripura, Assam, Jharkhand), militant politico-religious associations expressing their discontent and searching for a new nation (Jammu and Kashmir), Dalits and lower castes challenging Brahminism, and women asserting their distinctive voice. No wonder, grand ideologies like 'Hindu civilizational unity' or, for that matter, 'Indian nationhood' are questioned. Possibly this leads to a new way of seeing: seeing India as a series of fragments, not necessarily as a cohesive whole with a solid foundation. What are its implications? Identity politics is often seen as 'politically correct'. Because it is argued that identity politics leads to the democratization of our society; it has made us aware of pluralism, and compelled us to recognize differences. It challenges the hegemonic ideologies, and hence moves towards decentralization of power. While these achievements cannot be overlooked, there are, however, limits to identity politics.

First, as I wish to assert, it is *exclusivist* in nature. It tends to remain indifferent (if not hostile) to those who do not have a similar identity. As a result, it fails to appreciate the similarity of experiences that multiple and diverse groups may have in common. No wonder, in the absence of an adequate awareness of this linkage or connectedness, identity politics cannot have a broader humanistic agenda. It becomes narrow and limited in its perspective. It fragments and destroys what we otherwise need: a collective struggle for a just world. I wish to give two examples to make my point. To begin with, look at the politics of reservation. In recent times it has gained tremendous momentum because of the assertion of identity politics. But it also limits our perspective. While the marginalized castes strive for reservation, the forward castes condemn it, and attach 'stigmatized' identities to those gaining the benefits of reservation. This mutual hostility makes it difficult to recognize a shared zone—say, the zone of unemployment, irrelevant education, distorted development and oppressive agrarian practices—that seems to affect the destiny of all—poor Brahmins as well as poor Dalits. True, if we go by only statistics, the Dalits suffer more than the Brahmins. But life exists beyond statistics. Not all Brahmins are necessarily privileged. It is, therefore, important for all, irrespective of diverse identities, to come together, and fight for a just world. I am not privileging the economy over culture. Nor am I saying that the mode of humiliation of poor Dalits and poor Brahmins is exactly the same. I am aware that the Dalits suffer not just economically, but also culturally and ritually. The only thing I am arguing for is that we need to see beyond identity politics, and if we cannot broaden our horizon, people's struggles are bound to get crippled, fragmented and weakened. It is like saying that if Dalit politics remains merely Dalit politics, it cannot universalize itself. We should not forget that the beauty of a liberating politics is that it is capable of articulating itself as a shared aspiration for the larger society.

Likewise, look at the much talked about *uniform civil code*, and see how the constraints of identity politics make it difficult to strive for an emancipatory agenda for a healthy and egalitarian man–woman relationship. Those who are devotedly 'communitarian' suspect a modernizing state trying to interfere into the 'personal laws' of a religious community, because these laws are thought to be symbolizing its distinctive culture and identity. And the feminist organizations which are supposed to fight for women's equality get puzzled, because the assertive Hindu Right seeks to utilize this opportunity to further devalue the minority community. As a result, we witness silence, reluctance, or even diplomatic gestures: let the minority community decide for itself, and let the reform come from within! A bold and authentic struggle for an emancipatory man–woman relationship, as a result, becomes a distant dream. Because the logic of fragmented/exclusivist identity politics tells us that we can by no means be united. We are either Muslim or Hindu, Sikh or Christian. We are nothing beyond these identities!

My second criticism is that identity politics often falls into its own trap. It fragments itself, and, therefore, becomes self-defeating. Because there are identities within an identity, and as each of these identities wants autonomy, the result is a never-ending process of deconstruction. Look at, for instance, the North East—the ideal site of identity politics. Yes, we see a struggle for recognition, a struggle that seeks to differentiate the identity of a Mizo or a Naga from the imposed 'Indian' identity. But then, there are 75 major ethnic groups/sub groups, and 400 languages and dialects in the same region. And the inner conflict goes on: the dominant ethnic groups colonizing the marginalized ones. Hence we find the *Bodos* revolting against *Assamese* domination, the *Garos* against the *Khasis*, and the *Homars* and *Reangs* against the *Mizos*, the list is endless. Likewise, even though the lower castes see their common enemy in Brahmanism, the divisive nature of identity politics does not even spare them. No wonder, instead of a collective/ united struggle for a casteless society, we are witnessing the growing conflict between, say, the backward castes and the Dalits in Bihar and UP.

Third, identity politics has unintended consequences. True, it emerges out of an emancipatory urge to liberate the marginalized communities from stigmatized identities ('lower' caste, 'subdued' women, 'illiterate' tribe), and create a just society without any hierarchical principle. But then, there are ample historical evidences that demonstrate that the result of identity politics has often proved to be its opposite. In fact, the historically imposed identity, far from withering away, acquires a political meaning which is rather used in a purely instrumental fashion. Yes, I know that while I speak of the dialectic of identity politics, I ought to be careful. I am aware of an immensely sensitive (or sympathetic) reading of identity politics by contemporary social scientists. For instance, Javed Alam argues categorically that an appeal to caste for political mobilization does not necessarily constitute casteism (Alam, 2001). He reminds us that the battle for bourgeois equality in India is not being fought, as was the case in the West, between unequal individuals. It is being fought by the vulnerable communities which were collectively un-free. That is why, 'among the oppressed, the appeal to caste is for unification of similar *jatis* into larger collectivities and political mobilization for power so as to subvert the very relations of the varna order' (Ibid: 105). This struggle, as the politics of a Mayawati or a Laloo Prasad Yadav indicates, need not necessarily always follow the so-called civilized norms. But then, as Alam seeks to convince us with great care and sympathy.:

> The communities of the oppressed castes are now fighting for equality and recognition on the one hand, *vis-à-vis* the *dwija* castes and, on the other, against the privileges of the established middle classes. The battle is fierce and ugly: ugly because everyone among the oppressed is in a hurry and ready to jump the queue and break all the rules of the game so assiduously built up by us, the gentry. This is not to question the very worth of rules as such, but to recognize that to stick to rules assiduously is to wait rather longer in the queue, which is viewed as disadvantageous by the oppressed groups. We, therefore, must be cautious in judging by our sense of parliamentary decorum or social niceties, as much of the media and drawing room conversation does...(Ibid: 104).

Yes, Alam is right. We need to be cautious. We need not simply condemn identity politics. But what I am suggesting is far deeper. Identity politics, paradoxically, reinforces the same identity it seeks to transcend. No matter how sympathetic we are towards the 'progressive' role that identity politics has played, it is high time we became honest enough to acknowledge its crisis. It is good to be politically correct; it is equally important to be aware of the other aspects of identity politics. For instance, how often, because of the intensity of identity politics, one is persuaded to believe that one's identity itself can be a saleable commodity in the political market or a lucrative piece of academic consumption. One realizes that one's 'stigmatized' identity, paradoxically, has begun to give one 'privileges': the pride of being 'politically correct', or the immediate gains of reservation! As one falls into this trap of instrumental politics, one continues to retain one's 'backward' identity. One does not feel like transcending it, and evolving an alternative notion about oneself. No wonder, even Dalit elites would want their children to get reservation, and promote their 'Dalit' identities. It is indeed a paradoxical situation. One wants to end oppression and hierarchy. Yet, one finds oneself incapable of seeing beyond the existing typologies. One remains a Dalit, a woman, a Muslim. And the more one defines oneself through these categories (even if assertively), one reinforces the same hierarchical principle that constructs these oppressive dualities: Brahmin vs. Dalit, man vs. woman, and Hindu vs. Muslim. In fact, a major problem confronting our society is that we are trying to fight casteism through the categories implicit in casteism itself. Casteism, as a result, does not wither away. Instead, it becomes more and more conscious of itself. Even if I wish to see myself as humane (beyond all caste categories), the widespread identity politics would awaken my latent identity: I cannot be just humane. I would be told that I ought to be a Brahmin or a Yadav or a Dalit! The fact is that you and I need to redefine ourselves. The more we use the prevalent categories ('forward'/'backward'), and classify people on the basis of these stereotypes—even if for 'radical' purposes—the more we fall into the same trap. It becomes a vicious circle.

My final critique of identity politics is more serious in nature. I believe that identity politics, despite the 'progressive' role it plays, is not sufficiently demanding and challenging. Because it limits one's possibilities; it does not want one to expand one's horizon, and broaden one's universe. Instead, it dictates: 'Beware that you belong to a caste, a linguistic community, or an ethnic group, and you have to fight against 'others' in order to protect the rights of your group'. Seldom does it tell one that one is not just a Dalit, a woman or a Bengali; one is also a human being having multiple possibilities; one can, therefore, initiate a dialogue with others, and strive for a broader agenda that intends to liberate all. In fact, a great lesson of the Gandhian art of resistance, I have always believed, is that it is demanding and challenging. It wants me to have a dialogue even with my 'enemies', alter their consciousness, and create a shared world. No wonder, the meaning of decolonization, for Gandhi, was to liberate the colonizers as well as the colonized. Gandhi could, therefore, emerge as a huge banyan tree that could give shelter to all: a Christian, a Muslim, a Dalit, a woman, a poor peasant in Champaran, a textile worker in Ahmedabad, and even a bourgeois like G.D. Birla. In other words, the moral appeal of such an art of resistance is that it can universalize itself. The tragedy of identity politics is that it offers no such moral/ethical challenge. Instead, it is severely limiting in nature. It is also extremely possessive. It assumes that only the 'insiders' can speak for themselves; it fixes the 'outsiders', suspects them, and reproduces stereotypes. Imagine, for example, the damage that we cause to our search for truth when we say that 'Ambedkar is just a Dalit intellectual', or 'Gandhi is yet another forward caste reformer', or 'Marx is merely an European thinker', or 'Tagore is none other than a Bengali *bhadralok*.' The appropriation of certain symbols and icons, and exclusion of others go against the spirit of enquiry that seeks to negotiate, learn, and experience what hermeneutic philosophers would regard as the 'fusion of horizons'.

IV
Seeing Beyond Differences

The critique of identity politics, I am repeatedly arguing, does by no means suggest that our shared humanity is a 'homogeneous whole' without inner variations and differences. Unity is by no means uniformity. Meaningful unity, it has to be realized, emerges out of differences. And differences add colour to the world, make it exciting, beautiful and challenging. There are multiple varieties of plants, trees, flowers, mountains and rivers. Likewise, there are multiple forms of life. Let this multiplicity prevail. Even global projects that seek to transcend these barriers cannot overcome the diversity of identities. Well, there were many who once believed that modernity, because of its very nature, would universalize itself, and minimize cultural differences. Modernity, it was thought, would lead to similar aspirations, aptitudes and orientations throughout the world. With the irresistible process of modernization everywhere people would grow secular and rational, use the ever-expanding technological devices, celebrate science, attend schools, read mass-circulated newspapers, and exercise their voting power! In other words, it was thought that ascriptive/primordial identities and culture-specific differences would become secondary, and modernity would acquire a standardized universal face. History, however, demonstrates that this grand ambition centred on the expansionist/hegemonic character of modernity has not necessarily been fulfilled. It is, of course, true that modernity has helped breaking boundaries and barriers. Yet, the fact remains: societies have given distinctive culture-specific meanings to modernity. No wonder, as I have already argued, these days social scientists often speak of *multiple modernities*: modernities as shaped, articulated and redefined by divergent cultural/social histories. Look at our own case. Is our modernity similar to 'Western modernity'? Certainly not. In fact, a complex interplay of civilizational ideals and modernity, perpetual process of assimilation and synthesis have given a distinctive character to our modernity (Singh, 1996; Pathak, 1998). These differences can be understood better if we think of the following:

First, it is possible to take help of the instruments (i.e. technologies) of modernity without necessarily adopting a de-centextualized rationality. When I fall sick I can take modern medicine. Yet, I can go to a yoga teacher, and learn traditional healing practices. I may be computer savvy. Yet, I do not want to miss my Diwali or Id. In other words, I can retain my 'identity', even when I speak English, possess a credit card, and send my child to an American university to study nuclear physics. Call it whatever you like—compartmentalization or schizophrenia. The fact is that culturally shared memories and resultant identities refuse to wither away.

Second, modernity as it is practised creates a situation conducive to the assertion of traditional identities. A striking illustration is the politicization of caste identity in contemporary India. The process of modernization—democratization, mass mobilization, adult franchise, and use of political power for social upliftment—succeeds in organizing a caste group situated in diverse localities, and forming a political block. In other words, modern democracy, as our experiences suggest, is revitalizing the caste identity (Kothari, 1986; Rudolph and Rudolph, 1967). Likewise, we have seen that it is modernity—the quest for a centralized nation-state, and an ideology of unifying nationalism—that has given a distinctive meaning to religion. Far from existing as a spiritual faith, it becomes one's 'identity' which is used for mass mobilization, for consolidating the ideology of 'religious nationalism'. M.S. Golwalkar, to take a specific illustration, articulated this modernist spirit rather sharply (Golwalkar, 1939). He sought to convince his countrymen that all the five components of a modern nation—*geographical, racial, religious, cultural* and *linguistic*—could be seen in what he regarded as *Hindu India*. For him, here is a country with definite geographical unity, delimited by the sublime Himalayas on the North and the limitless ocean on the other three sides. Here is the ancient race—the Hindu race that professes the illustrious Hindu religion. Moreover, here is 'a culture which, despite the degenerating contact with the debased civilizations of the Mussalmans and the Europeans for the last ten centuries, is still the noblest in the world' (Ibid: .41). And finally, 'there is but, one language, Sanskrit, of which these many 'languages' are mere off-shoots' (Ibid: 67). In other words, for Golwalkar, modernity and religious nationalism are not incompatible with each other. As a matter of fact, what we are realizing is that modernity as it is practised does not necessarily have the power to make us memoryless. There are many narratives of modernity. The prevalent practice of modernity accelerates identities like caste, ethnicity and religion.

Likewise, globalization—the process that seeks to overcome national and territorial boundaries, and promotes large-scale cultural diffusion—is yet another important reality to reckon with. These days it is often argued that in the 'global village'—because of the unrestricted movement of transnational economic corporations, and remarkable innovations in information technology—it would no longer be possible to live in an isolated island, and retain an exclusivist identity. Instead, we are destined to live in a world in which the global market is bound to unite us! Yet, as I have mentioned in the earlier chapter, it is important to understand the limits to the process of a uniform global culture. The fact is that the 'global citizen continues to articulate himself/herself through distinctive national/ethnic cultural symbols and identities. Moreover, it should not be forgotten that asymmetrical globalization tends to arouse a deep-rooted anxiety: the fear of losing one's history, one's cultural memory and roots. We often see survival strategies used by people—say, diasporic communities—to safeguard their cultural identities. For example, Bengalis settled in America would not forget to celebrate their Durga puja, and organize a Satyajit Ray retrospective. And the story is not different for the other diasporic communities. Aparna Rayprol has studied this cultural dynamics among the Indians settled in America (Rayprol, 2001). She sees immense 'nostalgia' among the first generation Indian Americans. They visit the temples, and see themselves as part of a *gemeinschaft*.

> Regular visits to the home country as well as exposure to contemporary cultural products (such as the latest movies on video and fashion trends) enable immigrants to refresh their memories and to keep up with the changing cultural milieu back home...The Indian immigrants' desire for such things as the latest ethnic fashions, spices and specially foods, which they can easily acquire through global capitalism, is an example of nostalgia that is indeed embedded in consumerist culture (Ibid: 176).

Even among the second generation Indian Americans the question of identity is not altogether dead. As Rayprol reveals:

> All my respondents said that they have a respect for their parents' bilingual or multilingual skills and would like to improve their own Indian language skills. Many of them follow news about India in the media and on the Internet. Many young women like to wear Indian clothes for formal occasions. All of them love to eat Indian food, and some of them cook it, especially after they start living in campus-dorms (Ibid: 182).

In fact, what is interesting to note is that globalization also leads to the process of ethnicization. Yes, ethnic symbols get dislocated, marketized and packaged. Yet, ethnicization does indicate the search for a meaning—for an identity of one's own. It should also be remembered that globalization as a cultural homogeneity is often resisted. And this resistance, I have already indicated, might manifest itself in the revivalist/fundamentalist politics, or in the 'clash of civilizations'. In other words, identity politics does not die. It acquires a new meaning in the global era which is often characterized by unevenness, hierarchy and asymmetry.

Are we then destined to live with these identities and resultant differences without an unitary vision? As I am insisting, that is not the goal we should strive for. Differences are indeed important. But then, it is equally important to create a world that unites us. I, therefore, wish to see beyond the doctrine of differences. True, it has its emancipatory potential. It resists homogenization, pleads for multiple identities, and allows, particularly minority/marginalized cultures, to survive, But then, my anxiety that the doctrine of differences is not sufficiently equipped to teach us the lesson we all are waiting to be taught: Respect differences, but don't allow these differences to limit you. Retain your identity if you like, but don't forget to communicate with others in order to learn and unlearn, and create a shared world. In fact, we need an altogether fresh approach: a new way of thinking, believing and acting. I have already spoken of alternative modernity and symmetrical globalization. In continuity with these arguments, I wish to add the following:

First, it is important to create a social environment in which differences are not allowed to become hierarchical. Differences, we realize, make the world beautiful and exciting. Differences, however, become oppressive when these are graded and hierarchized. Take an example. Men and women are different—certainly biologically. Even though biology is not destiny, it may not be altogether impossible to have some differences in terms of their temperament, aptitude and orientation. And these differences are beautiful, and often arouse mutual admiration and attraction. The problem arises when these very differences are hierarchized, and when it is taught—through socializing practices—that men, as 'active doers', are intelligent and courageous, whereas women, as 'passive consumers', are inferior, irrational and sentimental. This hierarchy reinforces an oppressive patriarchal culture. No wonder, feminism interrogates this hierarchy, and, as some of its adherents would argue, equality is not sameness; equality is an assertion of reciprocal/symmetrical differences; equality means men and women realizing their shared human bond.

Living with differences without being hierarchical is not, however, an easy task. How often we feel tempted to denigrate others in order to assert the legitimacy of our own identity. We tend to assert that our nationality is more legitimate than theirs, our language is the best in the world, and there is no other religion like ours. The process goes on through education, family socialization, cultural beliefs and dominant stereotypes. That is why, pleading for symmetrical differences (as opposed to hierarchical differences) is also like pleading for an alternative mode of socialization. It requires the primacy of dialogue, not arrogance; and sensitivity, not indifference to others. At the same time, it is equally important to remember that the vision of symmetrical differences we are talking about needs to be sustained by concrete economic measures. The fact is that economic inequality often reinforces hierarchical differences. We have noticed how often women, Dalits, tribals and religious minorities get economically exploited. There is indeed a relationship between economic marginalization and one's stigmatized identity. The anguish of being marginalized/exploited often manifests itself through cultural politics—the politics of identity. That is why, if we are really serious about 'unity in diversity', we need to strive for a political economy that rests on the ethics of caring and the principle of distributive justice. The fruits of development need to be shared by all.

Second, I wish to argue that not all identities are necessarily desirable. We must be willing to discard those identities which are particularly oppressive and dehumanizing. For example, there is nothing wrong if one seeks to retain one's linguistic identity, and feels proud of, say, *Maithili* or *Bhojpuri* as a living language. Because this organic linkage with one's own language, so long as it does not degenerate into linguistic sectarianism, enriches culture and civilization. But one's caste identity, for example, is entirely different. It does by no means elevate our sensibilities. Caste identities, as a matter of fact, are terribly hierarchical; these identities dehumanize us, limit our possibilities, and go against the notion of a holistic and integral personality. None is disputing the fact that human personalities differ as far as their skills, aptitudes and orientations are concerned. It is also true that we cannot escape the division of labour, and it is quite likely that some of us would be oriented to scholarly pursuits, some would prefer worldly vocations, and some would excel as managers, administrators and warriors. But ascriptive caste identities are entirely different. Once I am born as a Dalit, I remain a Dalit forever, even if I am capable of learning, philosophizing and theorizing. Or, even if I am born as a Brahmin, I may have aptitudes for farming and agriculture. Caste, in other words, is a forced division of labour. It does not allow one to unfold one's real potential. Furthermore, it is restrictive and hierarchical. It privileges mental labour, and degrades manual endeavour. There is no reason to uphold caste identities. Moreover, it is important to think of and strive for a more balanced and integral personality. True, here is a world of specialization and heightened differentiation. Yet, there is an urgent need to reconcile the major faculties of one's being. For example, I may be a professor primarily working in the domain of knowledge and ideas. Yet, it should not prevent me from engaging in domestic work—cleaning my toilet, nursing my bedridden mother, and taking care of my garden. None of these activities is 'inferior' or 'impure'—which should be kept for 'lower' castes. Likewise, I may be a mechanic. In a good society it should not prevent me from seeing a *Bharatanatyam* programme, and helping my child in his school work. This is like Dalitizing the so-called Brahmin identity, and Brahminizing the so-called Dalit identity. I entirely agree with Arvind Sharma when he says that the caste system has become dysfunctional (Sharma, 1997:41–60). As Sharma argues, the division of society into four *varnas* might have been appropriate 'for an age when literacy was low and the main avenue for the acquisition of professional expertise was one's family'. But in our times, characterized by 'universal literacy' and 'global mobility', we have to think differently. For Sharma, we must realize that all the *varnas* are contained in every individual, instead of every individual being comprised within only one of the *varnas*.

It imposes a four-fold obligation on every Hindu:

1. As a Brahmana every Hindu must have minimal familiarity with the Hindu scriptures and rituals;
2. As a Kshatriya every Hindu must undergo compulsory military training as well as experience of political empowerment by participating in the political process;
3. As a Vaisya every Hindu must train for a profession, that is, undergo required vocational preparation and pursue a vocation; and
4. As a Sudra every Hindu must perform some form of manual labour or service (Ibid: 46).

The point I wish to assert is that we must be courageous enough to discard caste identities. The tragedy of Indian politics is that it reinvents caste identities, and paradoxically in the name of emancipating us from the caste system. Our politics and social science vocabulary need a new language that teaches one to see a man as a man, not as a Brahmin or a Dalit.

Third, it is important to accept that, despite having differences, we can work together, and constitute a shared public sphere. Let us think of the character of public institutions that we need to evolve. Imagine that I am a Bengali doctor working in a hospital. When a Mizo patient comes for medical treatment, I do not hesitate in giving my best to cure him. The spirit of working together transcends identity barriers and creates an institutional ethos that is humane and universal, not limiting to specific identities. Without this open character of public institutions, no shared culture is possible. None is denying the need for, say, specific institutions like schools and cultural centres for preserving specific cultural traditions and languages. But a mature society is one that steadily moves towards more open public institutions. It strives for a public space that experiences unity in multiplicity, and reconciles multiculturalism with shared humanism. In recent times sociologists have shown great interest in these institutions leading to the growth of a civil society (Beteille, 2000:172–97). Beteille, for instance, insists that the membership in these 'open and secular institutions' ought to be 'independent of such considerations as race, caste, creed and gender' (Ibid: 186). This is what is regarded as the 'culture of civility', and Beteille believes that in a country like ours where 'historical and demographic considerations require the co-existence of communities professing and practising different faiths and rites' we need this culture. The culture of civility, argues Beteille, is a 'culture of tolerance' (Ibid: 190). While agreeing with Beteille, I wish to add something more. We need tolerance, but not just tolerance. We also need a sense of humility. This implies that even if I have an identity of my own, I can learn from others, improve myself, and enrich the world. Yes, I tolerate differences. But I do something more. I learn from others, expand my horizon, and think of some kind of a consensus. I am an Indian. It is not my intention to cease to be an Indian. But my Indianness is fluid, flexible and accommodative. I should not hesitate to learn from, say, an African or an European. I love Hindi. Yet, I can learn from Bengali poetry. Learning from others, it must be realized, does not belittle one. Instead, what limits one is one's arrogance and conservatism. It is this willingness to learn which, I believe, would enable us to see beyond limiting identities, and create a shared world.

Fourth, as I wish to emphasize, it is equally important to evolve a distinctive way of seeing, and cultivate immense sensitivity so that we can experience and appreciate unity. It is easy to see differences; it is easy to quarrel, and say that you and I are different. Be it language, religion, dietary practice or social custom—everything is different. But it requires an extraordinarily high degree of *empathy* to realize what unites us despite so many differences. There are two aspects of this empathy. To begin with, I would mention its anthropological component. Let us concentrate on India. Yes, India is a site of differences and identity politics. Yet, if we are really willing to see, it is also a domain of unity. I am not just talking about the unity emanating from 'nationalist/modernizing' forces: Indian Railways, Indian Civil Service, Indian Army and Indian Cricket Team. I am talking about a deeper unity at the civilizational level. This unity, far from being a finished product, is essentially a process perpetually evolving and growing. One can notice this process in the rhythm of life, in village fairs, in folk cultures, in the constant interaction between classical and folk traditions, in religious pilgrimage, and interestingly even in popular Hindi films. I entirely agree with N.K. Bose, and borrow his language to describe this ongoing process of cultural unity.

> Whether on the banks of the Narmada or the Godavari or the Kaveri, or the confluence of the Ganga and Yamuna or of the Alakananda and the Bhagirathi the Bengali pilgrim learns to regard all the pilgrim centres in India as his own by offering prayers in the same Sanskrit language and participating in the same ceremonies. Not merely on account of the King's rule, but even more through the journeys of endless pilgrims across the ages, a kind of cultural unity has gradually emerged throughout the country. The same Ramayana and Mahabharata, and the same stories from the Puranas touch the sensibilities of people throughout... the society...There is a proverb in Hindi that flowing water and the roving *sadhu* are the best. The *sadhus* and *sannyasis* in moving from pilgrimage to pilgrimage, from village to village and across the different kingdoms have undoubtedly contributed something to the establishment of the cultural unity of India (Bose, 1975: 112).

While I speak of Indianness, my intention, I must clarify, is not to privilege an exclusivist Indian identity. Because that would be self-defeating. The idea is to transcend even Indianness, and experience a collective bond with the larger humankind. That is, as I have said in the earlier chapter, a meaningful path to symmetrical globalization: a process in which multiple national identities are engaged in an authentic cross-cultural conversation. I would repeat that this quest for something more broader, more inclusive and more universal does not mean that we have no roots. Yes, we do have roots. We have our languages, religions and nationalities. That is why, when I wish to be an Indian I do not cease to be a Bengali or, when I intend to become global I do not cease to be an Indian. But my Bengaliness or Indianness is only a cultural form or a social context that enables me to expand my branches into the sky. In such a world differences prevail, but differences are not limiting, hierarchical and exclusivist. Instead, a complex/dialectical interplay of unity and differences enriches the world. I believe Sri Aurobindo was visualizing a similar ideal of human unity when he wrote:

> The ideal of ultimate aim of Nature must be to develop the individual and all individuals to their full capacity, to develop the community and all communities to the full expression of that many sided existence and potentiality which their differences were created to express, and to evolve the united life of mankind to its full capacity and satisfaction, not by suppression of the fullness of life of the individual or the smaller community, but by full advantage taken of the diversity which they develop (Sri Aurbindo, 1977: 400).

And the second component of this empathy, I must add, is essentially spiritual. It is like realizing that beneath differences lies the deeper unity. It is in this context that, I believe, each of us is like *Svetaketu* waiting to be taught by *Uddalaka*. Let me repeat some of these lessons from *Chandogya Upanishad*:

> *Just, as my dear, by one clod of clay all that is made of clay becomes known, the modification being only a name arising from speech, while the truth is that it is just clay* (VI.1.4)
>
> *Just, as my dear, by one nugget of gold, all that is made of gold becomes known, the modification being only a name arising from speech, while the truth is that it is just gold* (VI.1.5)
>
> *Just, as my dear, by one pair of nail scissors all that is made of iron becomes known, the modification being only a name arising from speech, while the truth is that it is just iron* (VI.1.6).

Yes, it is this deeper realization of unity that sees beyond forms and differences, and makes our world a lovely place to live in.

Before We Conclude ...

At this juncture it is not difficult for my readers to guess what I am striving for. I critique modernity. But then, I am not anti-modern, or, for that matter, postmodern. Instead, I seek to humanize modernity. I wish to alter its self-perception, and make it more humble and reflexive. Although I see immense possibilities in the process of cultural globalization, I intend to resist its asymmetry and unevenness. I want to make it truly symmetrical and egalitarian. I adore differences emanating from multiple social identities. Yet, I do not want to romanticize and essentialize these differences. My urge is to broaden our horizon, and realize our shared humanity. I am only rediscovering and emphasizing what many have already pleaded for: openness, dialogue, symmetry, simplicity and humanness.

Yes, it is indeed a philosophic quest (or life-quest) for grand ideals. Here is a world characterized by aggressive modernity, uneven globalization and ruthless identity politics. But it has to be acknowledged that a meaningful journey to a better world is impossible unless we internalize and take these ideals as our guiding principles. We are aware that politics without such a philosophic quest becomes merely instrumental and violent, economics degenerates into a profit-making endeavour filled with unbounded desire, and everyday life becomes routinized, directionless and pleasure-seeking. As a matter of fact, we need to work in the domain of education to arouse sensitivity to this quest.

Education is not just literacy. Nor is it merely a technical skill. Education is about cultivating the mind, and generating immense sensitivity to the world. Education is the light of understanding that enables one to distinguish what is life-affirming from what is destructive, or what is merely an attractive packaging from what is authentic and enduring. Education is the art of listening: the ability to see beyond one's limited horizon, and experience the larger world in one's own being. Education is the urge to appreciate the rhythm of life, not to get carried away by technological spectacles. Education, in other words, is about calmness, about simplicity, and about love and deeper awareness. We are aware of a splendid discourse on education. Dewey and Tagore, Illich and Tolstoy, Gandhi and Freire—all great minds have sensitized us, and inspired us to rethink education. This book is not supposed to narrate this discourse. Nevertheless, I believe that it has become necessary for all of us to work in the domain of education, because without education there is no possibility of a just, humane and egalitarian world. Before I end this book, let me invite my readers to this exciting domain of social enquiry and life-practice.

References

Alam, Javed. 2001. 'Is Caste Appeal Casteism? Oppressed Castes in Politics' in Jodhka, Surinder S. (ed). *Community and Identity: Contemporary Discourses on Culture and Politics in India.* New Delhi: Sage Publications.

Ambedkar, B.R. 1987. *Philosophy of Hinduism* (Dr. Ambedkar's Writings and Speeches. Vol.III). Government of Maharashtra: Education Department.

______. 1998. "Gandhism: The Doom of the Untouchables' in Dallmayr, Fred and Devy, G.N. (eds). *Between Tradition and Modernity: India's Search for Identity: A Twentieth Century Anthology.* New Delhi: Sage Publications.

Appadurai, Arjun. 1990. 'Disjuncture and Difference in the Global Cultural Economy' in Featherstone, Mike (ed). *Global Culture: Nationalism, Globalization and Modernity.* London: Sage Publications.

Aurobindo, Sri. 1977. *The Human Cycle, The Ideal of Human Unity, and War and Self Determination.* Pondicherry: Sri Aurobindo Ashram.

Barber, Benjamin. 2004. 'Jihad vs McWorld', in Lechner, Frank J. and Boli, John (eds). *The Globalization Reader.* Malden/Oxford, Blackwell Publishers.

Bauman, Zygmunt. 1987. *Legislators and Interpreters: On Modernity, Post-modernity and Intellectuals.* Cambridge: Polity Press.

Beauvoir, Simon de. 1980. *The Second Sex.* London: Picador.

Benedict, Ruth. 1971. *Patterns of Culture.* London: Routledge and Kegan Paul.

Bennett, Oliver. 2001. *Cultural Pessimism: Narratives of Decline in the Postmodern World.* Edinburgh: Edinburgh University Press.

Berger, Peter L. Beger, Brigitte and Kellner, Hansfried. 1979. *The Homeless Mind.* New York: Penguin Books.

Beteille, Andre. 2000. *Antinomies of Society: Essays on Ideologies and Institutions.* New Delhi: Oxford University Press.

Bhaskar, Roy. 2002. *From Science to Emancipation: Alienation and the*

Actuality of Enlightenment. New Delhi: Sage Publications.

Biswas, Prasanjit and Bhattacharjee, Shukalpa. 2001. 'The Outsider, the State and Nations from Below: North East India as a Subject of Exclusion' in Azam, Kausar J (ed). *Ethnicity, Identity and the State in South Asia*. New Delhi: South Asian Publishers.

Bloom, Harold and Trilling, Lionel (ed). 1973. *Romantic Poetry and Prose*. New York:Oxford University Press.

Bolock, Robert and Thompson, Kenneth (eds). 1992. *Social and Cultural Forms of Modernity*. Cambridge: Polity Press.

Bose, N.K. 1975. *The Structure of Hindu Society*. New Delhi: Orient Longman.

Brass, Paul R. 1991. 'The Punjab Crisis and the Unity of India' in Kohli, Atul (ed). *India's Democracy: An Analysis of Changing State-Society Relations*. New Delhi: Orient Longman.

Buhler, G. 1964. *The Laws of Manu*. Delhi/Varanasi/Patna: Motilal Banarasidass.

Chandra, Bipan. 1988. *Indian National Movement: The Long-Term Dynamics*. New Delhi:Vikas Publishing House.

Chatterjee, Partha. 1986. *Nationalist Thought and the Colonial World: A Derivative Discourse*. New Delhi: Oxford University Press.

_____. 1994. *The Nation and Its Fragments: Colonial and Post Colonial History*. New Delhi: Oxford University Press.

Chomsky, Noam. 1989. *The Culture of Terrorism*. London: Pluto Press.

Coomarswamy, Anand K. 1982. *The Dance of Shiva*. Delhi: Munshiram Manoharlal Publishers.

Debord, Guy. 2001. 'The Commodity as Spectacle' in Durham, Meenakshi Gigi and Kellner, Douglas M. (eds). *Media and Cultural Studies: Key Works*. Massachusetts/Oxford: Blackwell Publishers.

Dube, Leela. 2001. *Anthropological Explorations in Gender Intersecting Field*. New Delhi: Sage.

Dumont, Louis. 1970. *Homo Hierarchicus: The Caste System and Its Implications*. Delhi: Vikas Publications.

Eisenstadt, S.N. (ed). 1987. *Patterns of Modernity*. Vol. I. London: Frances Pinter.

Feyerabend, Paul. 1978. *Science in a Free Society*. London: Verso.

Foucault, Michel. 1982. *Discipline and Punish: The Birth of the Prison*. Middlesex: Penguin Books.

Friedman, Jonathan. 1999. *Cultural Identities and Global Process*. London: Sage Publications.

Fromm, Erich. 1982. *To Have or To Be*. London: Abacus.
Gandhi, M.K. 1927. *An Autobiography or My Experiments with Truth*. Ahmedabad: Navajivan Publishing House.
_____. 1989. *Hind Swaraj or Indian Home Rule*. Ahmedabad: Navajivan Publishing House.
Giddens, Anthony. 1990. *The Consequences of Modernity*. Cambridge: Polity Press.
Golwalkar, M.S. 1939. *We or Our Nationhood Defined*. New Delhi: Manohar.
Griffith, Ralph T.H. 1971. *The Hymns of the Rig Veda*. Vol. I–II. Varanasi: The Chowkhamba Sanskrit Series Office.
Gupta, Dipankar. 2000. *Mistaken Modernity: India Between Worlds*. New Delhi: Harper Collins.
Hasan, Joya (ed). 1994. *Forging Identities: Gender, Communities and the State*. New Delhi: Kali for Women.
Hayward, Tim. 1994. *Ecological Thought: An Introduction*. Cambridge: Polity Press.
Hobsbawm, E.J. 2004. 'The World Unified' in Lechner, Frank J and Boli, John (eds). *The Globalization Reader*. Malden/Oxford: Blackwell Publishers.
Husain, S. Abid. 1985. *The National Culture of India*. New Delhi: National Book Trust.
Huntington, S.P.1996. *The Clash of Civilizations and the Remaking of World Order*. New Delhi: Viking/Penguin.
Ilaiah, Kancha. 1996. *Why I am not a Hindu: A Sudra Critique of Hindutva Philosophy, Culture and Political Economy*. Calcutta: Samya.
_____. 2004. *Buffalo Nationalism: A Critique of Spiritual Fascism*. Kolkata: Samya.
Inkels, Alex. 2000. 'Making Men Modern: On the Causes and Consequences of Individual Change in Six Developing Countries' in Roberts, J.T. and Hite, A. (eds). *From Modernization to Globalization: Perspectives on Development and Social change*, Blackwell / Massachusetts: Oxford.
Jameson, Fredric. 1984. 'Postmodernism or the Cultural Logic of Late Capitalism', *New Left Review*. Vol. 146 (July–Aug): 53–92.
Jan Nederveen Pieterse. 1995. 'Globalization as Hybridization' in Featherstone Mike, Lash Scott and Robertson, Roland (eds). *Global Modernities*. London: Sage Publications.
Kakar, Sudhir. 1981. *The Inner World: A Psycho-analytic Study of Child-*

hood and Society in India. New Delhi: Oxford University Press.

Kher, Martin. 2001. *Rethinking Globalization: Critical Issues and Policy Choices*. London/New York: Zed Books.

Kishwar, Madhu. 2004. 'No to trade, yes to aid'. New Delhi: *Indian Express* (19.1.04).

Kothari, Rajni (ed). 1986. *Caste in Indian Politics*. New Delhi: Orient Longman.

Kothari, Rajni, 1995. 'Under Globalization: Will Nation-State Hold?', *Economic and Political Weekly* (July 1, 1995).

Lerner, Daniel. 2000. 'The Passing of Traditional Society' in Roberts, J.T. and Hite, A. (eds). *From Modernization to Globalization: Perspectives on Development and Social Change*. Blackwell/Massachusetts, Oxford.

Madan, T.N. 1983. *Culture and Development*. New Delhi: Oxford University Press.

_____. 1996. 'Anthropology as Critical Self-Awareness' in Seth, D.L. and Nandy, Ashis (eds). *The Multiverse of Democracy: Essays in Honour of Rajni Kothari*. New Delhi: Sage.

Marcuse, Herbert. 1966. *One Dimensional Man: Studies in the Ideology of Advanced Industrial Society*. Boston: Beacon Press.

Marx, Karl and Engles, Fredrich. 1975. *Manifesto of the Communist Party*. Moscow: Progress Publishers.

Marx, Karl. 1977. *Economic and Philosophic Manuscripts of 1844*. Moscow: Progress Publishers.

Matilal, Bimal Krishna. 1988. *Confrontation of Cultures*. Calcutta: K.P. Bagchi and Companies.

_____. 2002. *The Collected Works of Bimal Krishna Matilal: Ethics and Epics* (edited by Ganeri, Jonardon). New Delhi: Oxford University Press.

McGuigan, Jim. 1999. *Modernity and Postmodern Culture*. Buckingham/Philadelphia: Open University Press.

Mead, G.H. 1934. *Mind, Self and Society: From the Standpoint of a Social Behaviiorist*. Chicago: The University of Chicago Press.

Nandy, Ashis. 1983. *The Intimate Enemy: Loss and Recovery of Self Under Colonialism*. Delhi: Oxford University Press.

_____. 1987. *Traditions Tyranny and Utopias: Essays in the Politics of Awareness*. New Delhi: Oxford University Press.

_____. 1994. *The Illegitimacy of Nationalism*. New Delhi: Oxford University Press.

Negus, K.1992. *Producing Pop: Culture and Conflict in the Popular Music*

Industry. London: Longman.
Nehru, Jawaharlal. 1983. *The Discovery of India*. New Delhi: Jawaharlal Nehru Memorial Fund.
_____. 1984. *An Autobiography*. New Delhi: Jawaharlal Nehru Memorial Fund.
Nisbet, Robert. 1967. *The Sociological Tradition*. London: Heinemann.
Omvedt, Gail. 1994. *Dalits and the Democratic Revolution: Dr. Ambedkar and the Dalit Movement in Colonial India*. New Delhi: Sage Publications.
Oommen, T.K. 1997. *Citizenship, Nationality and Ethnicity: Reconciling Competing Identities*. Cambridge: Polity Press.
_____. 2004. *Nation, Civil Society and Social Movements: Essays in Political Sociology*. New Delhi: Sage Publications.
Packard, Vance. 1982. *The Hidden Persuaders*. New York: Penguin Books.
Parekh, Bhikhu. 1989. *Colonialism. Tradition and Reform: An Analysis of Gandhi's Political Discourse*. New Delhi: Sage Publications.
Pathak, Avijit. 1998. *Indian Modernity: Contradiction, Paradoxes and Possibilities*. New Delhi: Gyan Books.
_____. 2002. *Social Implications of Schooling: Knowledge, Pedagogy and Consciousness*. New Delhi: Rainbow.
_____. 2004. 'Teaching/Learning Sociology: A Critical Engagement with Modernity', *Sociological Bulletin*. January–April 53 (1): 31–48.
Pusey, Michael. 1987. *Jurgen Habermas*. Chichester, London: Ellis Horwood Ltd/Tavistok Publications.
Radhakrishnan, S. 1953. *The Principal Upanishads*. London: George Allen and Unwin Ltd.
Raychaudhuri, Tapan. 1986. *Three Views of Europe from Nineteenth Century Bengal*. Calcutta: K.P. Bagchi.
Rayprol, Aparna. 2001. 'Can You Talk Indian? Shifting Notions of Community and Identity in the Indian Diaspora? in Jodhka, Surinder S. (ed). *Community and Identity: Contemporary Discourses on Culture and Politics in India*. New Delhi: Sage Publications.
Robertson, Roland. 1995. 'Globalization: Time-Space and Homogeneity-Heterogeneity' in Featherstone, Mike, Lash, Scott and Robertson, Roland (eds). *Global Modernity*. London: Sage Publications.
Roszack, Theodore. 1972. *Where the Wasteland Ends: Politics of Tran-*

scendence in Postindustrial Society. New York: Doubleady and Company.

Roy, Arundhati. 2004. 'Do turkeys enjoy thanksgiving?' New Delhi: *The Hindu* (18.1.04).

Rudolph, L.L. and Rudolph, S.H. 1967. *The Modernity of Tradition: Political Development in India*. Chicago/London: The University of Chicago Press.

Saberwal, Satish. 1996. *Roots of Crisis: Contemporary Indian Society*. New Delhi: Sage Publications.

Said, Edward. 1973. *Orientalism*. London: Routledge and Kegan Paul.

_____. 1994. *Culture and Imperialism*. London: Vintage.

Sangari, Kumkum and Vaid, Sudesh (eds). 1989. *Recasting Women: Essays in Colonial History*. New Delhi: Kali for Women.

Sarkar, Sumit. 1985. *A Critique of Colonial India*. Calcutta: Papyrus.

Schumacher, E.F. 1983. *Small is Beautiful: A Study of Economics as if People Mattered*. London: Abacus.

Sharma, Arvind. 1997. *Hinduism for Our Times*. New Delhi: Oxford University Press.

Shourie, Arun. 2004. 'The Reforms Mandate—Part II'. New Delhi: *Indian Express* (5.2.04).

Singh, Yogendra. 1996. *Modernization of Indian Tradition*. Jaipur: Rawat.

_____. 2000. *Culture Change in India: Identity and Globalization*. Jaipur/New Delhi: Rawat Publications.

Singh, K.S.2002. *People of India: Introduction*. New Delhi: Oxford University Press.

Sklair, Leslie. 1991. *Sociology of the Global System*. Hertfordshire: Harvester Wheatsheof.

_____. 2004. 'Sociology of the Global System' in Lechner, Frank J and Boli, John (eds). *The Globalization Reader*. Malden/Oxford: Blackwell Publishers.

Stiglitz, Joseph. 2003. *Globalization and Its Discontents*. New Delhi: Penguin Books.

Tagore, Rabindranath. 1985. *Nationalism*. Madras: Macmillan.

Thompson, John. 1995. *The Media and Modernity: A Social Theory of the Media*. Cambridge: Polity Press.

Tibi, Bassam. 2004. 'The Challenge of Fundamentalism' in Lechner, Frank J. and Boli, John (eds). *The Globalization Reader*. Malden/Oxford: Blackwell Publishers.

Tolstoy, Leo. 1967. *On Education*. Chicago/London: The University of Chicago Press.

Uberoi, J.P.S. 2002. *The European Modernity: Science, Truth and Method*. New Delhi: Oxford University Press.

Urry, John. 2003. *Global Complexity*. Cambridge: Polity Press.

Weiner, Myron. 2001. 'The Struggle for Equality: Caste in Indian Politics' in Kohli, Atul (ed). *The Success of India's Democracy*. Cambridge: Cambridge University Press.

Willson, Michele. 1997. 'Community in the Abstract: A Political and Ethical Dilemma?' in Holmes David (ed). *Virtual Politics: Identity and Community in Cyberspace*. London: Sage Publications.

Index